"A smart, witty guide to business recovery and development, packed with real-world insights and innovative strategies for success."
Mike Keep, Business Founder and Entrepreneur

"David's book distils mastery into simplicity, making the complex seem effortless while highlighting the transformative impact of experience and strategy in business growth."
Alexandra Garcia, Head of Sustainable Business Development

"David is a wonderful human being whose depth of intense real-world experience is thoughtfully analysed and generously shared here to help others shortcut to success."
JP Hamilton, Director, World Wide Generation

"David has a considered approach to business turnaround and transformation. Every business is unique, but his process uncovers where the real and unperceived problems lie."
Stephen Dimon, Director, 1st Group Ltd

THE 7 PILLARS

Strategies for Business Breakthrough

Copyright ©2024 David Parry

Apart from any fair dealing for the purposes of criticism or review, as permitted under Copyright, Design and Patents Acts 1998, this publication may only be reproduced, stored or transmitted, in any form or by any means, with prior permission in writing of the publishers, or in any case of the reprographic reproduction in accordance with the terms of licences issued by the Copyright Licensing Agency. Enquiries concerning reproduction outside these terms should be sent to the publishers.

PublishU Ltd.

www.PublishU.com

All rights of this publication are reserved.

With thanks to all my friends and colleagues worldwide, without whom these stories would not exist.

Most of all to my dear children, Chris, Anna, Ryan, and Jessica, who have gracefully endured the late nights, extended travels, and the many missed birthdays due to their ever-absent father. Your resilience and love have been my anchor and a source of endless inspiration. To you, I owe more than words can express.

I love you all dearly.

Preface

In the ever-evolving landscape of modern business, agility and innovation have emerged as the keystones of success. Companies that excel today approach challenges with a proactive and holistic mindset. As a seasoned founder and Managing Director of a Market Research Organisation, my journey has intersected with over two hundred large B2B clients, guiding them in harnessing crucial data to enhance metrics like Average Order Values and Upsell opportunities and in identifying significant events to prevent Churn.

My association with David, author of 'The 7 Pillars' has given me a front-row seat to his remarkable expertise in navigating the complex realms of business growth and recovery. David's unique ability to orchestrate holistic improvement is nothing short of inspiring. One notable example was when he assisted a struggling international technology services group in revitalising its sales strategy, resulting in a 150% increase in their Year-Over-Year revenue — a testament to his impactful methodologies.

'The 7 Pillars' is not just a narrative of David's forty year journey in transforming underperforming businesses into success stories. It is a treasure trove of practical wisdom for anyone: from budding entrepreneurs to seasoned executives. David's engaging storytelling illuminates the path of resilience and adaptability, ensuring readers experience numerous enlightening moments. His insights are more than just theoretical musings; they are actionable strategies that have proven effective in the real world.

As you delve into the pages of this book, expect to find a blend of inspiring stories and hands-on advice that will equip you to navigate your own business challenges. Whether you're looking to inject new life into a stagnant business or scale new heights in a flourishing one, 'The 7 Pillars' promises to be a guiding light.

I wholeheartedly encourage you to embark on this enlightening journey.

Mike Keep, Business Founder and Entrepreneur

Author Page

A Journey in Business and Values

My business recovery and development career began early, evolving into international business and the dynamic world of conglomerates. This is where I developed a keen interest in global business recovery strategies. I realised that all businesses adhere to fundamental principles despite varying sizes and products.

The highlight of my career has been solving intricate business challenges and collaborating with diverse teams. This experience was enriching, watching teams flourish through these efforts. However, my perspective shifted when I observed short-term profit strategies leading to job losses, conflicting with my belief in sustainable growth. This prompted me to start my own business, focusing on a more balanced approach to success without relying on aggressive, asset-stripping methods.

I learned that while business growth is process-driven, building a cohesive, motivated team is challenging and rewarding. My professional life, marked by highs and lows, taught me the transient nature of wealth and power, contrasting with the enduring value of faith, family and compassion.

Notable achievements include revitalising a failing manufacturing business in my twenties and fostering growth at an organisation for people with disabilities, underscoring the importance of humility and respect.

I find immense joy in uniting diverse individuals in an international setting and celebrating the richness of varied cultures and perspectives.

My family alongside values like honour, truth and kindness lie at my core. A growing belief in a Higher Power guides my personal and business paths, leading me toward a more empathetic and sustainable approach to corporate success.

Contents

SECTION 1: Introduction

SECTION 2: The Seven Pillars of Sales Performance

    Pillar 1: Strategy and Planning

    Pillar 2: Sales Management

    Pillar 3: Sales Process

    Pillar 4: Organisation and Development

    Pillar 5: Knowledge and Skill

    Pillar 6: Sales Enablement and Technology

    Pillar 7: Sales Channels

SECTION 3: Mastering Sales Strategies, Dynamics and Personal Growth

SECTION 4: Why Businesses Fail

SECTION 5: Understanding the Business Coaching Logic

Conclusion

About the Author

DAVID PARRY

SECTION 1:
Introduction

In a world where business success often treads a fine line between brilliance and madness, established businesses invariably fail not because of external market forces but because of poor leadership and internal resistance to change.

However, imagine standing at a crossroads of an international business where the paths to unprecedented success or stagnant performance are many and complex. This is the dilemma many entrepreneurs and executives face – a quest for a breakthrough amidst overwhelming odds.

In this book, I unveil the transformative power of the '7 Pillars' framework, a strategy honed from years of helping steer underperforming businesses towards remarkable success. Witness how innovative leadership, united teamwork and a willingness to embrace change led to $395 million in combined revenue growth across my client portfolio within just two years of implementation.

The '7 Pillars' go beyond theoretical concepts; they offer a proven, practical and reliable roadmap to success, underpinned by real-world results and compelling stories of resilience and adaptability.

Once you find yourself firmly planted in the "adult" phase of life, you're bound to encounter situations that defy all reason. For me, this often meant attending various social gatherings — little parties, dinners, mixers — populated by a curious mix of individuals. Some were friends of friends, others distant acquaintances I'd struggle to place unless given a lengthy, detailed backstory. As a single dad, the art of mingling at these events often involved a delicate balance of being amiable while internally debating if I could sneak a glance at the emails on my phone without seeming rude.

The true test of endurance, however, came when the conversation well ran dry. Inevitably, someone would launch the age-old icebreaker, barely more thrilling than commenting on the weather: "So, what do you do for a living?" It's a tedious dance but a familiar one. And when that topic was exhausted, there was always the fallback of sporting allegiances to navigate. Having been around the block, I knew these routines well enough, bracing myself for the predictable rhythms of polite, yet uninspired, chatter.

Having navigated enough social soirées, I've become well-versed in the conversational tango that follows introductions. My response to the inevitable "What do you do?" — "I'm an international business consultant" — usually prompts a mix of blank stares and awkward nods. They imagine me in a suit (spot-on), jet-setting across the globe (also true), but that's where their assumptions hit a roadblock.

Some might speculate that I'm a covert operative (think International Man of Mystery, minus the mystery and the international intrigue) or maybe a closeted billionaire (a notion my ex-wife might have found particularly amusing). But in reality, my job is more straightforward yet puzzlingly complex.

I'm the guy who fixes broken businesses.

Of course, it's not as simple as it sounds. If it were, this book would be unnecessary, and I'd probably be mastering the art of flipping burger patties instead. The challenge lies in the uniqueness of each business. Like individual snowflakes or people's wildly varying opinions on the latest chart-topping tunes, every business is a distinct entity. Each one presents its own labyrinth of challenges, goals, hierarchies and invariably, a colourful ensemble of characters. Some are allies, others have obstacles, but all are a source of fascination as I weave through their business cycles, unravelling the mysteries of where their well-intentioned strategies derailed.

With more than a few decades under my belt, it's easy to talk about my career with a certain degree of confidence. But it wasn't always that way. I didn't exactly stride into this profession as much as I stumbled across it.

I'll be the first to admit that my origin story doesn't include me getting a giant dose of gamma radiation, taking a superhuman serum to fight the bad guys or even coming from a planet with a different coloured sun. But it does tell a lot about what brought me here and if you're going to go on a journey with me through the process of turning businesses around, I want you to know me better, see what makes me tick and develop a little bit of trust and transparency going forward.

So let's jump into the time machine, double-check the flux capacitor and zoom back in time half a century or so to see how it all started for me.

Back Then

Before my foray into business recovery, there were the days of my youth marked by adventures that seemed worlds apart from the corporate challenges I would later face. After leaving university, well after my brief stint as a wannabe rock star, I went into teaching. More specifically, teacher by day and a somewhat less-than-glamorous van driver by night. It all started with a noble quest to supplement my teacher's salary, which was, let's say, more passion-driven than financially rewarding. I joined forces with my brother in this side hustle, commandeering four-tonne box vans for a local automotive group. Our mission? To deliver medical supplies across the UK's quaint but comically narrow tree-lined lanes and rolling countryside, often too narrow for such vehicles (the trees frequently won).

Imagine us, two young men in their 20s, in these hulking vans filled to the brim with cough medicine and other pharmaceutical goodies. One of our more "aromatic" adventures involved a cargo of cough syrup. If a bottle broke, and they did, the van transformed into a makeshift aromatherapy spa — though I wouldn't recommend *eau de cough syrup* as a scent to dab behind your ears before a hot date.

Fate intervened in my life on a day when we were transporting pharmaceutical samples to a major company's sales conference. Because we were young and thought we were masters of time and space, we arrived, fashionably late, to a scene straight out of a sitcom. The marketing director, red-faced and frazzled, came out to greet us, only to find his precious samples playing dominoes in the back of our van. He wasn't thrilled and ordered us out of his sight as quickly as possible. It turned out that was quite fortuitous for yours truly because a few years later, I was hired by the same company with him as my direct superior. Fortunately, the delivery lorry instance was far back enough in the past to keep him from connecting the dots, clearly to my advantage!

Our driving escapades weren't just about playing delivery boys. We also dabbled in the high life, driving a white Rolls-Royce and a BMW 7 series, ferrying ladies to their glamorous evenings out. There we were, two young lads, living it up as makeshift chauffeurs. It was like being in a James Bond movie, only with less espionage and a distinct lack of toothbrushes that turned into radios, or belt buckles that could spray poison gas.

But not all our tales were about glitz and glamour. Take, for instance, the Great Glasgow Brake Parts Odyssey. It was a mission dubbed "critical": Deliver these parts by day's end or face automotive doom. So off I went, embarking at an ungodly hour, only to arrive at a closed factory eight hours later. Turns out, "urgent" in factory terms meant, "We'll see you Monday!"

After hours of waiting, negotiating, and a tad of bribery, the parts were offloaded – a process involving forklifts, sleepy workers and me playing an impromptu game of "tie the chain around the pallets." By the time I finished, it was 02:00 and I had to choose between sleep and a heroic drive home. Heroism won, but my truck had other plans, breaking down amidst the Glasgow nightlife.

Enter my saviour, a Scotsman walking home late at night as merry and inebriated as they come. He graciously offered to help by taking me home and got his wife out of bed so that she could prepare some food and the warmest cup of tea. She was pleasant throughout the whole thing, but I imagine he slept on the couch for at least the next week after that slight imposition on her beauty sleep.

Eventually, we found an all-night garage in the Gorbals district of Glasgow, and I finally bunked on the floor of a garage that definitely wasn't featured in any travel guides.

Since I didn't recall 007 ever sleeping on the floor of a 24-hour garage to thwart S.P.E.C.T.R.E or meeting any exotic double-agents while loading pallets well past midnight, I decided that it might be time to trade in the dynamic 1-2 punch of apple polisher and delivery driver for something a little more long-term and stable.

As I mentioned previously, my first job after school

teaching was in pharmaceuticals and my first boss had mercifully not recognised my face. I wasn't in any position to save businesses yet, but I did get a crash course in what was then cutting-edge marketing. I found myself rubbing elbows with some very sharp minds, both in and out of the company. At one point, I spent six months pounding the pavements of London, selling ad space in a medical journal for GPs. This is my first experience with the infamous London Underground during rush hour – an experience I enjoyed as much as a root canal. It would not so joyfully be repeated until two decades later when we set up the technology marketing business in the UK.

One of the funniest moments I recall was when we merged with another pharmaceutical company that produced dental hygiene products. Picture a roomful of ten marketing and product gurus, all eagerly trying out our latest creation – a dental plaque-revealing toothpaste. Sounds great, right? Until everyone's mouths and lips turned a dazzling shade of neon pink. We're talking a full week of looking like we'd all kissed a flamingo. Not exactly the best look for professional meetings!

Life kept turning up unusual coincidences from there. After three years in pharma marketing, I was offered the position of group marketing director for another firm; incredibly, it was the finance and automotive leasing group where I had worked nights as the anti-James Bond.

I had originally been engaged by the group to tighten up and improve their marketing activities, but after about six months I overheard a conversation about the closure of the manufacturing company. I tried to persuade the owners that I could help them rescue the company from collapse. They were sceptical because I knew nothing about manufacturing. So I decided to appeal to a few of their less professional behaviour traits by offering my services in the form of a bet. If I could turn the business into profit within six months, they would let me drive one of their supercars from the vehicle leasing company. If not, I would forfeit fifty percent of my fees. It probably speaks a few volumes about their financial strategy that they were willing to gamble with a six month employee, but at the time, all I cared about was winning the bet and proving my talents were legitimate.

Time for a little number crunching, then.

The manufacturing company's original turnover was less than two million dollars and it had been losing money each year for the previous three years, which was why the group owners planned to close it.

On the other side of the equation was me, a twenty-seven year old with much more ego than actual experience.

Located in an industrial estate, our facility housed around twenty young employees, led by an equally youthful foreman. The factory, chaotic and teeming with metal and wood product manufacturing equipment, lacked organisation, training protocols, and essential safety measures. Sales were sporadic, relying primarily on internal group references and word-of-mouth.

Our initial step was to implement structured and safer work practices. This not only minimised waste but also boosted morale and significantly decreased the likelihood of accidents. By negotiating better deals for raw materials and waste management, we transformed the factory into a more efficient, safer, and cleaner environment.

These improvements alone were sufficient to steer the business towards profitability – or at the very least, away from losses – within the first six months. But our ambitions didn't stop there. Over the next several years, we exponentially grew the business into a seven million dollar enterprise with an impressive eighteen percent net profit margin.

Thinking back, to make it grow was all about, what these days we would call account-based marketing, without the benefit of social media or the internet, of course. Mailing prospects was literally that: a physical mailer that went in the post, coupled with good old-fashioned shoe leather that went out and met with people.

Needless to say, I won the bet and was soon zipping around in the supercar. The more I learned, the more I hungered for more knowledge. That led me to dive into learning and development, pursuing a Diploma from the Institute of Marketing, various sales training programs and even a certified accountancy and finance diploma. My foray into finance was sparked by my initial bafflement at how the Group Chairman always seemed to know our month-end sales and profit figures before I did. Initially, I attributed this to his superior financial acumen. However, it turned out his method was much simpler: by asking me weekly about factory shipments, he could estimate our profits based on the average value of these shipments. This experience was a powerful reminder that sometimes, the right questions can lead to straightforward yet valuable insights.

I learned some hard-hitting truths about business recovery. For instance, I realised the power of promoting your business even when it seems like no one is listening. In those early Monday morning meetings, the message was clear: manage your cash flow effectively or risk your position. I learned to focus on key performance indicators (KPIs), often in unexpected places, including that tracking the number of truckloads leaving the factory was a more accurate measure of business health than many traditional metrics. Targeting the right audience with a laser-focused message was another key takeaway. It wasn't just about broad marketing; it was about understanding and speaking directly to the needs of your specific audience. I learned the importance of building a diverse and skilled team where each member brought something unique to the table. This approach fostered innovation and allowed us to tackle challenges from multiple angles.

But the road wasn't always smooth. I faced numerous challenges and made mistakes along the way. There were high-risk situations, like high-stakes pool games and undocumented business dealings, which taught me the darker aspects of business. The importance of workplace safety, regulatory compliance and ethical practices became glaringly obvious. I also saw firsthand the consequences of straying from these principles – broken relationships, personal turmoil and legal battles. It taught me persistence in the face of obstacles, the importance of timing in sales, and the need for excellence in everything. Trust became a central theme; trust in people, but with the understanding that accountability and measurement were key to success. These lessons were hard-earned, often accompanied by personal sacrifice and ethical dilemmas. Ultimately, this journey was more than just about turning a business around. It was a profound lesson in understanding the complexities of business, the human element in corporate decisions, and the fine balance between risk and reward.

Ironically, a journey that began with a struggling light commercial vehicle components company led to multiple business recovery scenarios in more than forty countries. I find myself always wanting a new challenge to conquer. They all haven't been winners – more on that later – but they have been chock full of teachable moments, life lessons, and essential building blocks to get me to the next phase of understanding how things work. Along the way, I've met some highly successful people who have played an essential part in bringing about these achievements. It is always a learning experience, always something new. We all work differently from each other, whether it is how you sell in the US, how the Northern Europeans manage customer accounts or the importance of personal relationships in Asia and the Middle East.

Over time, I've become part of a group of highly successful folks who've grown their businesses. We all come from different parts of the world — France, England, the US, Canada and even as far afield as Hong Kong and China. It's all different types of companies, all different sizes, industries and locations. It's a struggle for a typical modest Brit to admit they've helped companies go to $8 million from $3 million, let alone to $120 million from $60 million! There's not some magic pill that allows me to guide companies from Point A to Point B. Typically, I am engaged as an interim manager or director and I have a process in place that lets me pull back the curtain and see what's really going on behind the scenes. Regardless of what it is, the biggest thing to impress on every company at that point is to get them onboard with the idea of (drumroll, please):

Change Management

It takes time. That's the one thing that's always true when you're trying to effect change — don't give up.

To succeed, we need to understand what happens on the ground floor. That is one of the critical things apart from understanding why a business is not performing. Sometimes the obvious questions are the ones that businesses simply do not ask or don't know how to find an answer for. This is often because they are too close to it – forest for the trees thing. Other times it's because they don't want to ask the question because they already suspect the answer and don't want to admit it; like they over hired and need to lay people off, or they've worked forever on some process that isn't working and probably need to scrap it. It is important to create a team of people inside the organisation who want to bring about change, believe it is possible and are prepared to try to achieve it.

Your first three months will be figuring out what's wrong, figuring out what your plan is and then implementing it. You are beginning to see change in your next three months. If you're an expert in this kind of thing, at least in sales, you might see your numbers change and take off like a rocket in nine to twelve months.

An expert will get stuff done faster and more efficiently, but anyone can achieve the same type of success; they just have to be patient. The most important thing of all is measurement. If you don't have the KPIs, you can't see what's happening. Get the right people in the right jobs. Recruit them properly and onboard them properly so that they're ready to go to battle with you. That's the big, big boulder that needs fixing in most businesses I work in. That's the moment.

Top-shelf leadership is important, but who you really need are the heads of the business units. They are the ones that have to deliver it at the front end. As an interim, you still have to get involved with the details, working with individual salespeople or teams from different functions.

You are trying to create that appetite and momentum for change. This is especially true in businesses that have been underperforming. It may be that the business is tired of trying and not getting anywhere, or the present management does not know how to break through the barrier, so they start to micromanage and threaten the workforce with being fired unless they bring in better results. Of course, this simply makes for an even less motivated and underperforming workforce.

Most companies that hire me invariably ask when the change will happen. It depends on the size of the business and the level of complexity. That can be a vexing answer for some, but this is not a cookie-cutter, one-size-fits-all business.

The key takeaway is that change takes time and patience, which does not necessarily mean slow — indeed, far from it. We need to have the businesses focus on getting the right people in place and providing the necessary support and resources for success.

SECTION 2:
The Seven Pillars of Sales Performance

Some years ago, I was introduced to the Capability Maturity Model (CMM) used in software development. That was the lightbulb moment that enabled me to carry out in-depth analysis of a sales operation more accurately than a simple numerical diagnostic survey and in a fraction of the time that it would take manually. A key finding in the CMM was that we were able to see a pattern to areas of sales operation that had the greatest impact on sales performance.

Business performance is complex, but from the sales perspective, seven key areas of performance emerged as the most common areas which determined success or failure.

1. Strategy and Planning
2. Management
3. Process
4. Organisation
5. People Knowledge and Skill
6. Sales Enablement
7. Sales Channels

Let's call these the 7 Pillars of Sales Performance and within that the three "P's" are the most important: Planning, Process and People.

Individual companies will have distinctly different performance levels, but the core areas and sub-criteria remain the same. Understanding this led to what became a repeatable and proven methodology for business recovery and growth for me.

The key to significant revenue improvement is to take a "whole business" approach to creating a bespoke solution. This means that a company needs to understand not only the causes of its current underperformance, but also how to measure the extent that each one is a problem. Because of this need for accuracy, the CMM is ideal. It means we can create very explicit standards at every level to describe the current state and quality of sales operations, competency, and the potential for continuous improvement. These key drivers and performance criteria are each measured against a capability scale. This allowed us to deliver a systematic first in-depth understanding of where a business is now, where they want to get to and measure the gap, looking at future capability and not just historic performance. By benchmarking internal and external performance, it generates a unique assessment of future sales capability. Within the structure of the seven major areas of sales performance, there are forty-five critical success criteria and almost three hundred points of reference scenarios to identify a sales team and wider stakeholder current performance levels.

Understanding the seven pillars is vital to understand business recovery. While this next section will include some "heavy lifting", I've included some real-life case studies and a good sprinkling of humour throughout as well to keep you learning and listening.

Pillar 1: Strategy and Planning

The first of our seven key pillars of performance improvement is Strategy and Planning.

US President Dwight D. Eisenhower emphasised from his military experience that "plans are for nothing, but planning is everything."

There are numerous examples of companies I have worked with which have shown varying levels of best practice in relation to strategy and planning – some more successfully than others.

However, *without exception, the high-performing companies always carry out thoughtful strategic planning and implementation roadmaps. Equally without exception, the companies that failed or at least underperformed did not.*

Some were weighty tomes and others simple one-page executive summaries supported by measurable activity roadmaps. It does not really matter which route is taken as long as there is one that is shared, understood by all and reviewed over time.

The effective execution of business goals, strategy, planning and policies can create exceptional performance. Conversely, inefficiencies or neglect in tracking can precipitate potential sales and profit losses. This section delves into the nuances of this pivotal process.

A high benchmark score in any domain indicates an organisation's well-defined strategy, which resonates clearly and consistently with its staff. In harmony with the company's vision and value proposition, such a strategy guarantees uniform excellence in customer service delivery. Conversely, a score below the benchmark in these areas suggests that your business might not leverage its full potential, risking significant revenue and profit losses. The ensuing guidelines aim to highlight key focus areas for bolstering performance.

A big part of planning begins with an optimal vision statement that harmoniously balances growth and change while remaining steadfast to the company's desired impact and core values. It should be lucid and well-communicated to strengthen the brand and product offerings. Intimately linked to this is the company's value proposition. Scoring high in this arena shows an organisation's commitment to regularly refining its vision and value proposition, ensuring alignment with customer experiences. These elements are articulated effectively to fortify the brand and product offerings. Underperformance in vision and value proposition can spawn numerous challenges. An ambiguous vision may sow confusion over company objectives and priorities, blunting focus on key initiatives and stunting growth. A disjointed value proposition could lead to erratic branding and messaging, hampering the establishment of a robust brand identity. Additionally, a murky vision and value proposition can misguide employees and stakeholders, leading to misaligned decision-making and decreased efficiency. This situation could also impede the attraction and retention of top talent. A vague value proposition makes engaging customers challenging, adversely affecting customer loyalty and market share.

One of my favourite stories about the effects of a lack of vision for an organisation comes from a friend who worked State-side for a British-owned chemical news bureau. They thrived on price reports, insider information and real-time news reporting through paid subscriptions. Very little they put out was free to the public, so you knew it had to be top quality to charge people an arm and a leg for all the subscriptions. The editorial side of the company was all about brevity, correctly realising that its customer base was not paying money for long, flowing narratives but rather for the facts about a certain product and what its impact would be on their own companies or their investment possibilities. Keep it short, keep it simple.

That's why my friend and, well, almost every single one of his coworkers, was laughing to the point of crying when the big boss one day announced a new vision for the company that he had spent several weeks concocting. It was a single word: Boundarylessness.

That's right. The company that focused on brevity,

had decided that a sixteen-letter word that may or may not even exist was going to be its mantra for the future. The big boss didn't see the problem as he explained their capabilities to go beyond what existed now. He put the word on signs and placards all over the office and gave a couple more speeches about it. You can imagine how much space it took up. You can also imagine the response it got from a group of elite journalists who pride themselves on taking what has been said in thirty words and getting it down to eight or nine. Not a single person was inspired by it, not a single person changed their work ethic because of it and when the occasional visitor would come to the office and ask about it, most would say they didn't know what it was or that it was there when they started. Whatever amount of money and time had been spent by the big boss to create and launch this vision had been a complete waste.

Your company vision should act as a beacon throughout the business journey, especially in guiding the sales and marketing teams to effectively identify, secure, retain and expand your customer base. As the essence of your company, this vision must be articulated clearly across all levels, reinforcing your product or service proposition and brand. The value proposition, targeting your customers, is critical to your sales and marketing strategy. It succinctly outlines how your product or service resolves customer challenges and the benefits they can expect. Essentially, it tells customers why they should choose your business over competitors.

Sales and profits might decline if your sales team and channel partners falter in conveying this message. Regularly revisiting the value proposition with your sales and marketing team is crucial, as is engaging in role-playing exercises to demonstrate its effective communication.

Case Study: International Teamwork

The meeting in the client's head office in the north of the UK wasn't due until four o'clock, but there were people I needed to see and decided to leave at six o'clock for the three-and-a-half-hour drive to the north. Arriving early, the supercars were all lined up as symbols of corporate accomplishment. I said my "hellos" and found a corner to catch up on some emails.

The Chairman's personal "money minder" looked harassed. He was having a bad morning as someone wanted millions from the boss's bank account. The boss was on a boat in the Bahamas and no one wanted to disturb him. There were more phone calls and threats from one of the other directors. A subsidiary company seems to have a catastrophic cash-flow issue and needs money fast — before two o'clock. "Or else!" screamed another director. The money-minder was bereft of all sensibility and stormed off in disgust. It was like something out of a gangster movie.

They had decided that I should join the European

acquisition, which was not performing well.

This is the story of remarkable people from multiple countries across Europe, working hard, having fun and achieving far more than an incredible business turnaround, building a community of friends that has stood the test of time beyond just former work colleagues.

Led by a charismatic Frenchman, with a small team at the centre and highly capable country managers, we first came together to create a thorough and detailed recovery plan that became the cornerstone around which each country did its part.

Naturally, we did all that might be expected in sharpening up processes from recurring income licence fees in one country to better vendor management and continuous training and development of the sales and marketing teams in others.

However, while planning and process are key to business growth and recovery, the people element made this business quite unique.

The plan set out to double revenues in mainland Europe and deliver eighteen percent net profit within the next three years. One-third of this would come from introducing the group technology portfolio, with the balance from strengthening and expanding existing vendor products.

This plan was set against declining revenues, margins and loss of market share across Europe. The strategy was to benefit from the acquisition through product integration in both directions and creating a Europe-wide Infrastructure.

At the outset, we created a small management team, drawn from the group and European business, with a brief to drive up business performance whilst aligning business systems and processes to allow for a European rollout of the wider group products and services.

Detailed financial analyses and models were created. However, the key position at the start was a business with revenues running about eighteen percent down on budget. Margins were also down on the previous year, which meant that with increasing costs and a decline in revenues the business was at best breakeven against a budget of five percent net profit. Immediate short-term gains were quickly achieved through productivity improvements in local business focus, re-organisation, motivation, process definition and key performance Measurement against our recovery plan. Ongoing business performance improvement would be gained largely through integrating the current localised businesses into a cohesive European Group.

The new management team had focussed on short-term business performance improvement measures as well as defining a strategy to deliver future growth and profitability. Although there was still much to do, these actions were already showing positive improvements in business performance and, importantly, people's motivation throughout the regions.

In practical terms we took several immediate remedial actions including:

- Process improvement and performance measurement,
- Sales and Product planning,
- A daily focus on sales drivers, activities, KPIs and benchmarking,
- Goals and targeting with compensation schemes,
- Portfolio rationalisation,
- European Market analysis.

Outside these direct business measures, it was clear that the business needed to come together as a cohesive team and apart from almost continuous travel from country to country, we introduced quarterly business meetings "somewhere in Europe." These sessions were about planning and progress but also included a lot of fun and team building. Off-roading in the desert, meetings in Milan, canoeing in the Dutch canals or camping in a "not-so-five-star" Bedouin tent in the North African desert complete with resident scorpion, will forever be a lasting memory. You have to remember that while everyone is there to work, they are also people who want to enjoy what they are doing. If you can get them into a situation where they can do both, you will help everyone succeed in the long run.

Customer Segmentation

A top-quartile score indicates a company's commitment to systematic performance reviews, Voice of the Customer (VoC) surveys and additional research to optimise or expand sectors. The organisation showcases a clear, well-understood approach to account segmentation implemented across the sales team. This strategy ensures timely and efficient delivery of products or services.

Customer Experience

At the heart of every business lies the customer experience: a critical factor in today's highly competitive and demanding market. Achieving a top-tier score in customer experience reflects a company's proficiency in identifying and consistently fulfilling customer needs with high-quality solutions. Moreover, such companies engage in efficient, continuous client feedback mechanisms, like regular customer surveys and user forums, to perpetually refine their customer service. By embracing professionalism and well-defined strategies, companies can elevate from being good to truly exceptional in customer service. However, companies struggling in customer service may encounter significant hurdles affecting their overall success. A damaged reputation, fuelled by negative reviews and a diminished brand image, can hinder new customer acquisition and retention. Moreover, diminished customer loyalty might push clients towards competitors, decreasing customer lifetime value and repeat business.

Inadequate customer service can also impede a company's growth and expansion efforts. Addressing customer grievances and rectifying poor service issues can be costly and time-consuming, diverting focus from strategic initiatives. Furthermore, employees lacking empowerment or the necessary tools to deliver exemplary customer service may experience low morale, leading to higher turnover rates and reduced productivity. To counter these challenges, companies must prioritise customer service by investing in training, implementing effective feedback systems and regularly reviewing service strategies for ongoing enhancements.

Understanding the nuances of customer preferences is crucial. Do customers value the uniqueness and quality of your products or services, or are they more price-sensitive? How do they weigh factors like quality, customer care and responsiveness? Often, customers can be incredibly forgiving if they feel well-treated and their expectations are surpassed.

To attain customer service excellence, establish a clear strategy and process. Whether formalised through Service Level Agreements (SLAs) or informally as part of your business ethos, these commitments to excellence in customer service should be unequivocally communicated. Encourage all employees to contribute to exceptional customer service. Evaluate how internal interactions and attitudes impact customer service delivery. Aim to make your company not only easy to do business with, but also a pleasure, fostering a culture that champions customer service excellence.

Marketing

High benchmark performance here is a testament to the exceptional quality and effectiveness of a company's marketing efforts. This level of achievement is often marked by an in-depth understanding of the company's vision, strategy, market segmentation, and ideal customer profile. Effective communication channels ensure that marketing efforts are precisely targeted at the most appropriate prospects. It never ceases to amaze me how tone-deaf people can be for how their most likely customers want to be communicated with. I think this every time I see a commercial like denture cream during an afternoon block of "Bluey" on Disney Jr. or companies that have no business appealing to young people trying to get hip with campaigns on Instagram.

Outstanding performance in marketing is characterised by a seamless integration of marketing and sales planning, activities and performance measurement. A dedication to continuous improvement is evident, underpinned by regular internal communication and feedback from the sales team. This collaborative approach between marketing and sales is instrumental in driving consistent success and growth. Conversely, a company underperforming in marketing may face several challenges. Inadequate targeting due to a poor grasp of the company's vision, strategy and customer profiles can lead to inefficient use of resources and missed opportunities. This situation may be exacerbated by a lack of synergy between the marketing and sales teams, leading to disjointed efforts and strategies. Moreover, the absence of regular communication and feedback from the sales team can leave the marketing department without the crucial insights needed to refine and optimise strategies.

Before the Internet, sales and marketing were often like two ships passing in the night; both were convinced they were doing their job well and that the other camp was the one who couldn't handle their business. They didn't exactly become best friends forever when technology weaponised them to start working together, but they are at least aware that synergy between them equals success for both parties. This gap can limit the effectiveness of marketing campaigns. Without a commitment to ongoing improvement, marketing strategies may become outdated, reducing efficiency, customer engagement, and overall business performance. Addressing these issues requires companies to enhance their marketing activities and foster a culture of collaboration and continual improvement.

The interplay between marketing and sales is pivotal for driving sales and overall business success. If sales teams report subpar results, it's imperative to reassess the alignment and effectiveness of marketing activities in relation to sales objectives. Effective collaboration between marketing and sales ensures proper targeting and engagement with the right prospects and customers. Understanding the distinction between marketing-qualified leads and sales-qualified leads is essential for refining lead generation and nurturing processes.

Marketing's role in creating a conducive environment for engaging prospects and supporting sales initiatives — including account management, customer advocacy, and retention strategies — is crucial. For optimal business performance, marketing and sales must actively collaborate, setting measurable goals, objectives, and establishing robust feedback mechanisms. This collaborative spirit enables both teams to understand and leverage leads more effectively, thereby continuously enhancing their collective efforts.

Pillar 2: Sales Management

High performance suggests more than just competency; it reflects a mastery of sales management. These managers shine in establishing clear goals, coaching their team to cultivate essential sales and business skills, and synergistically working towards the organisation's financial goals. Conversely, underperforming sales management can unravel a company's fabric, leading to unclear goals and priorities, confusion and a scattered focus. The lack of guidance, training and support limits employees' potential, hampering performance.

Ineffective sales management can demotivate employees, dampening team morale and sales performance. There is very little that demoralises people at work more than coming to the realisation, or at least having the opinion, that your boss doesn't know what they are doing. It's akin to the first time you're watching your favourite sports team and you realise that you're older than the head coach and it's painfully obvious he or she doesn't know what they're doing. Poor resource allocation further exacerbates the issue, hindering the organisation's strategic and efficient resource allocation. Weak sales management creates an environment lacking accountability and performance tracking, making it challenging to pinpoint areas needing improvement.

Addressing a lagging sales team involves scrutinising management practices. The sales manager's role is pivotal — from recruiting and onboarding to developing and motivating the team. They must direct the team's focus towards suitable customers and prospects. Effective sales management is about conducting meaningful sales meetings that offer learning and growth opportunities, not just progress reports.

Continual assessment of the team's performance, identifying improvement areas and providing necessary support are part of a sales manager's repertoire. Setting clear expectations, offering constructive feedback and nurturing a collaborative and positive work environment are keys to unlocking the team's potential. Investing in the team's professional development and well-being can dramatically elevate the organisation's performance and success.

Case Study: Global Major Account Management

This business in question was renowned for its technical sustainability software capability and almost three hundred Blue-chip global accounts in its portfolio. It had a small business development team led by a very capable sales director and a handful of customer service people in the UK, Hong Kong and the US.

Thanks to a charismatic CEO and Chairman, coupled with their highly skilled technology founders, the business had achieved global notoriety and was ahead of its time. Although it operated in the world of sustainability, its leadership saw themselves as software developers rather than sustainability experts. "We are not tree huggers; we sell software," was one infamous saying in the business.

A global US corporation eventually acquired it to help clients solve their critical business challenges and prepare for future opportunities. Although they had successfully built an enviable customer portfolio, there had been little focus on upselling or cross-selling deeper into the client base with other product offerings. The company was considering raising investment to finance growth and its focus was to grow sales to existing customers. Its pricing model included licence and day-rate sales, intending to increase recurring licence income and consequent business value. However, licence sales accounted for less than thirty percent of annual revenue at that time. A new business team focused on acquiring new customers, but no one was responsible for managing or growing the existing accounts other than the small customer service team. That was Trouble with a capital "T" and needed to be rectified as soon as possible. The challenge was to build and train new teams of people in Chicago, the UK and Hong Kong – all capable of understanding how to engage and grow business within major global accounts.

We created a new recruitment and induction process, and training programme to speed up the effectiveness of recruits, coupled with a module learning programme enabling account managers to demonstrate the company's complex sustainability software solutions and modules. We also created customer user group workshops, segmented by industry, and increased sales productivity by refining customer and sales journey workflows.

Within six months, we had coached, recruited and developed a competent major account management team with improved account management and sales skills. Pipeline growth was up by a stunning eighty-one percent with a higher mix of module licence recurring income sales. Customer administration and technical support, measurable account management sales processes, sales pipeline activity and customer advocacy programmes were provided, alongside in-depth customer analysis, account segmentation and major account planning.

We delivered individual and team sales best practices, coaching workshops, and implemented activity based KPIs and performance tracking, with individual sales targets, 1:1 coaching and personal development plans. In preparation for the company's ultimate sale, we conducted a complete sales and customer audit and negotiated a realignment of all global customer agreements.

Growth continued strong and by the end of the second financial year of our involvement, we had far exceeded the original expectations, more than doubling revenue and, importantly, growing licence sales to fifty-two percent from thirty percent of revenue. The impact within two years was to see the number of customers grow from two hundred to three hundred – a fifty percent increase, with upsell revenues and recurring income multiplied three times in the same period.

Sales Methodology

Top-performing sales methodologies are more than just processes: they are dynamic systems that leverage data and cutting-edge technology, ensuring sales team members are well-equipped and knowledgeable. Organisations that perform highly in this area don't just follow a set pattern; they are constantly reviewing and refining their methodologies based on customer feedback, maintaining a consistent sales approach and prioritising their team's skill enhancement. They're like a great rock band, constantly reinventing itself. Like the Beatles. By the time all their imitators were doing the three-minute songs about how swell they thought a girl was and how they'd like to kiss her on the cheek, George, Paul, John and Ringo were telling us about Penny Lane, and Elanor Rigby, and how somebody was the Walrus for some reason.

Staying ahead of industry trends and fostering a culture of continuous improvement positions these organisations for enduring success. An underperforming sales methodology, falling in the median-to-lower quartiles, can spell serious challenges. The absence of a cohesive, current approach can lead to ineffective strategies, missed opportunities and declining revenue. Neglecting continuous improvement and industry trends can render a company unable to adapt to evolving customer needs and market shifts. A deficient methodology can sap the sales team's productivity and motivation, impinging on the company's overall performance and growth potential. Poor customer relationships may develop when sales representatives lack the tools and skills for meaningful engagement, jeopardising customer loyalty and the company's reputation.

Investing in a robust, consistent sales methodology aligned with industry best practices is crucial to rise above these hurdles. Providing ongoing training and support boosts performance and fosters stronger customer relationships. Implementing one or two well-defined methodologies is a vital first step. Introducing a consistent, best-practice approach, coupled with comprehensive training and regular review based on customer feedback, can markedly uplift sales performance.

While flexibility is essential, a shared understanding of the best approaches for your business and effective customer engagement is crucial. Encourage practice and role-playing to refine skills and techniques. Apply these methodologies in real interactions, learn from successes and failures, and continuously refine your approach based on these insights. The right sales methodology should be tailored to your business needs and sales environment. Whether a classic or more contemporary approach, the right methodology can drive improved results and help your sales team excel.

Pipeline Management

Efficient pipeline management is a cornerstone of optimising an organisation's resources, expertise and skills to maximise sales results. High performance in this area reflects an acute awareness of the pipeline's significance, with regular reviews of sales processes and conversion metrics informed by customer feedback. These organisations maintain consistent pipeline visibility, management and processes that resonate with customer requirements, leading to fruitful sales outcomes. Attuned to the dynamics of the sales pipeline, they adeptly adjust strategies, ensuring steady progress towards sales targets. Low performance in pipeline management can lead to inefficient resource use, missed opportunities and reduced revenue. Inaccurate sales forecasts and difficulty pinpointing improvement areas often accompany poor pipeline management.

It's surprising how often companies, regardless of size, overlook the importance of understanding their sales pipelines. Insights into the pipeline's size, shape, conversion ratios, and timing are vital for evaluating sales performance. The sales pipeline is a barometer for sales opportunities at different stages and probabilities. As opportunities progress, a portion inevitably drops out at each stage. Monitoring and analysing the pipeline enables more informed decisions, identifies bottlenecks, and optimises sales strategies. Maintaining a robust sales pipeline is essential for consistent target achievement. Some opportunities might stall or disappear, necessitating a larger volume at the pipeline's early stages to meet sales targets. The challenge lies in accurately determining the required deal volume and value at each pipeline stage to hit sales targets consistently. Management must have clear visibility of the pipeline's quality, efficiency, and effectiveness. By meticulously monitoring and analysing the pipeline, organisations can pinpoint improvement areas, adjust strategies and maintain a steady flow of deals, driving revenue growth.

Forecasting and Quotas

Accurate sales forecasting is an art that requires meticulous and consistent monitoring of the sales pipeline, scrutinising opportunities at every stage, from prospect to conversion. Scoring highly in this area reflects an organisation's prowess in fine-tuning its forecasting processes — these are not merely routine checks but strategic reviews enhancing the quality, efficiency and precision of forecasts. Such processes yield reliable, actionable metrics for the sales team and management. Mastering sales forecasting allows organisations to allocate resources adeptly, accurately predict revenue growth and make strategic decisions that propel business success forward.

Median-to-low performance underlines the critical need for precise forecasting, directly influencing your company's ability to meet sales quotas and foster growth. If sales forecasts consistently miss the mark and the sales team underperforms, the sales pipeline is the first place to seek improvements.

Sales pipeline management is the cornerstone of crafting accurate sales forecasts. Organisations can significantly refine their forecasts by meticulously monitoring the customer journey and understanding the position, approximate value and duration of opportunities at each sales stage. Prioritising this aspect of sales performance is essential for any organisation aiming for growth and success.

Enhancing performance involves a data-driven

approach: consistently measuring, tracking, and analysing the sales pipeline across individuals, teams, and the company. This approach helps identify disparities in knowledge, skills, and activities, paving the way for targeted improvement strategies. By rigorously examining the sales pipeline and performance metrics, organisations can uncover areas ripe for enhancement. A more accurate and effective sales forecasting process can emerge with focused effort and time, propelling overall sales performance and fostering robust growth.

An organisation lagging in sales forecasting faces misallocated resources, unmet revenue targets, and challenges in making informed strategic decisions. Tackling these issues involves several critical steps. First, enhance data collection and analysis – ensure the sales team consistently logs information about leads, prospects, and sales opportunities in a centralised system like a CRM. This practice offers a clearer view of the sales pipeline.

Second, establish clear sales stages and criteria by defining steps in the sales process and specifying criteria for advancing leads or prospects. Standardising the forecasting process helps identify improvement areas more easily. Investing in the sales team's sales forecasting and pipeline management training is crucial. Encourage open communication and collaboration between sales and other departments, such as marketing and finance, to align everyone with shared objectives. Additionally, implementing forecasting tools and technology, including sales forecasting software, AI-driven analytics and CRM integrations, can automate and streamline the forecasting process.

Your team should continuously review and adjust its forecasts. Regular updates based on actual results and evolving market conditions will help maintain a more precise and current understanding of sales performance and potential.

Performance Management

Optimal sales performance management is a multifaceted endeavour, pivoting on adept people management, streamlined process design, comprehensive sales enablement and integrated technology systems. Excellence in this domain extends beyond the sales organisation, reaching out to channel partners and customers wherever possible.

The crux of best practices in sales performance management lies in cultivating a continuous learning and improvement culture. This culture fosters growth, adaptability, and constant enhancement across all business functions, including sales. Implementing integrated performance metrics and assigning ownership to relevant stakeholders allows an organisation to monitor progress and pinpoint areas needing refinement effectively.

Suboptimal performance in sales management is often marked by disjointed people management, inefficient processes, inadequate sales enablement and poorly integrated technology systems. These deficiencies typically don't extend beyond the organisation's walls, further impeding growth and success. A culture of continuous learning and improvement is usually absent in such settings. Processes stagnate, the collaboration between various business functions, including sales, is minimal, and without integrated performance metrics or clear ownership, tracking progress and addressing performance gaps becomes challenging.

Achieving optimum performance starts with a robust recruitment, selection and induction process, identifying individuals who align with your team and business values. Post-recruitment, establishing a culture of personal development planning, coaching, training, and progress monitoring, augmented by effective targeting and motivational compensation plans, is paramount. High-performing organisations understand that employee engagement and inspiration are key to extraordinary results. Developing and retaining talented salespeople is vital for your company's financial health and future success. Since turnover among salespeople is typically high, ensuring they feel successful and supported is crucial to reducing turnover.

A data-driven approach to sales performance management is essential for effective planning, forecasting, territory mapping, incentive design, and ongoing analysis, all aimed at maximising performance. Identify key performance metrics and assess how your CRM and other systems can provide automatic, real-time performance data. Consider who will use this information and how it will be managed. Evaluate how your team defines and implements best practices across the sales organisation and their alignment with your business vision, goals, and objectives. Also, consider territory management, quotas, and compensation plans to create a comprehensive sales performance management strategy.

Relying on spreadsheets and unaligned systems will invariably lead to inefficiency and, most likely, subpar performance and limited achievement.

Policies and Compliance

Running any business requires guidelines or policies universally understood and adhered to. *For a sales team to reach peak performance levels, having guidelines for everything from recruitment to deal initiation and closure, to prospect selection and fostering customer advocates, is imperative.* These policies and guidelines are embodied in a sales playbook in high-performing sales environments. This modern tool is not the outdated sales manual of yore but a dynamic, online repository of sales best practices and business processes tailored to each customer scenario. Continually updated and refined, the sales playbook is an invaluable resource for all salespeople and channel partners, arming the team with the knowledge needed for success.

If your team has a performance average or below, underperforming in this area could stem from the lack of clear guidelines or policies. Perhaps the toughest part of this equation is that many people don't want to be told how to sell. They have their own unique formulations and strategies and will blanche when they are told to get in line. But it's your company and your investments, so it should also be your way or the highway when it comes to the overarching strategy.

Salespeople might be navigating without a compass, unsure of best practices, and thus, struggling to perform consistently across various sales scenarios.

To rectify this, consider developing a comprehensive sales playbook, that details sales policies, guidelines and best practices. This playbook should be easily accessible and regularly updated, enabling salespeople and channel partners to stay informed and aligned with the company's strategies. It guides sales teams through every stage of the customer journey, from prospecting to closing deals, onboarding, customer management, and advocacy. A comprehensive playbook should include:

- Step-by-step best practice guidelines for every stage of the sales process,

- Procedures for proposal creation, feedback gathering, and handling tenders, RFIs, and RFPs,

- Clearly defined quotas, activity expectations, compensation plans, and performance benchmarks,

- Organisational structure, job descriptions,

recruitment processes, and induction programs,

- Detailed territory allocation strategies,
- Personal development plans and training programs,
- Reporting requirements and meeting protocols,
- Intelligence on customers and competitors, including battle cards for reference.

A well-crafted playbook supports sales best practices and is invaluable for new hires and channel partners, speeding up the onboarding and learning process. It provides a consistent benchmark for top performance and guidance on achieving success for larger or global teams. Efficient onboarding and sales enablement lead to quicker sales returns, underscoring the importance of maintaining an up-to-date and effective playbook.

Pillar 3: Sales Process

Sales is a process; if it is not a process, it is a fluke.

Sales processes are not just a series of steps; they are the lifeblood of successful customer engagement, encompassing vital activities, content requirements, KPIs and timelines that guide buyers and sellers through the sales cycle. These processes should seamlessly integrate within the sales function and with marketing, sales operations, service and delivery. The cornerstone of an effective sales process is an in-depth understanding of the customer journey, informing and shaping the corresponding sales journey.

A top-quartile performance in this area signifies that your organisation has mastered designing sales processes that provide robust governance yet remain agile enough to adapt to diverse opportunities, customers, markets, or channels. These processes are the backbone of accurate forecasting and foster an environment of continuous learning and improvement for the sales team, facilitating regular updates and modifications as required. They consist of specific steps and distinct activities, embedding sales methodologies into the very fabric of your workflows. While these processes are designed with a chronological mindset, they remain flexible, avoiding the pitfalls of rigidity or strict sequential completion. Conversely, poor sales processes and workflow performance might indicate several underlying issues. The sales processes could be unclear, outdated, or too rigid, hindering the sales team's ability to adapt and respond effectively to varying scenarios. Ineffective workflows can obstruct accurate forecasting, leading to missed sales targets and a lack of insight into the customer journey. But not every sales strategy is created equally.

Case Study: Acquire, Recover, Sell

In the early nineties, back when dinosaurs roamed the earth, people had phones that lived in their cars and we all thought the best songs on earth were tunes like "Macarena" and "Who Let the Dogs Out." I became part of a major international conglomerate that extended its operations across Europe, beyond just the UK. This enterprise was focused on acquiring businesses, usually valued between $20-50 million dollars and above.

Its strategy was straightforward: it would rapidly cut costs and then accelerate growth to increase profits. This approach typically led to reselling the acquired businesses at a profit, often within a year to eighteen months.

The group CEO relied on a particular set of financial ratios, which he always kept neatly folded on a small sheet of paper in his wallet. These ratios were uniformly applied across various businesses and industries to guide cost-cutting, often leading to significant layoffs. This relentless pursuit of efficiency and profit underpinned the core ethos of their operations.

Initially, joining this international mergers and acquisitions team was an exhilarating learning experience. However, as time passed, the repetitive nature of the job and the ethical concerns it raised – particularly regarding layoffs and aggressive profit strategies – started to trouble me, raising questions about the sustainability and morality of such a business model.

One particularly notable experience included a French manufacturing company with five factories and approximately seven hundred and fifty employees, specialising in steel storage solutions. This part of my career journey stood out as unique as it was my first time with an international business. I had been invited to become part of the senior mergers and acquisition team, including a charismatic Scotsman who, though quietly spoken, commanded the respect and love of us all. We were joined by a highly capable and experienced German director, a senior PA who was second in command to the MD and kept us all on track, and our guru strategist from the UK, who became my significant mentor. My role included managing the marketing, product management and sales teams.

Our main office was nestled in the seventeenth Arrondissement of Paris and we resided in an aparthotel situated picturesquely along the Boulevard de Clichy. The Moulin Rouge was a stone's throw in one direction, theoretically offering nightly escapades, and a church stood behind us, conveniently located for those moments of repentance after indulging a little too much in the Parisian nightlife.

For two years, our routine was a weekly London-Paris shuttle. We'd catch the first flight from London City Airport to Orly on Monday mornings and return on the last possible flight on Friday nights. This often involved a frantic dash through the infamously chaotic French traffic, exacerbated by our MD's penchant for leaving it until the eleventh hour. Back then, the concept of a smoke-free office hadn't quite made its way across the English Channel. Entering the boardroom often felt like diving into a cloud of "Gauloises" cigarette smoke – a corporate smog. Sometimes, stepping into the MD's office was like entering a foggy abyss; seeing him through the smoke haze was a challenge in itself, a situation that practically came with a future health warning.

The main office housed around fifty people, with the rest scattered across factories throughout France. Sales were decent, but not quite at the level of our ambitions. We spent many hours coaching the French sales team, who would nod in agreement during meetings and then, with a quintessentially French flair, seemingly forget everything as soon as we left the room. Despite this, we managed to drive significant growth, thanks in no small part to our marketing and product management teams. They were wizards in market and competitor research, crafting detailed sales playbooks and innovating new products as effortlessly as a Parisian chef whips up a soufflé.

My French language skills were initially a challenge, but I quickly found a solution, embarking on "language learning" strolls through the streets of Paris each morning with Jacques, a tutor whose patience was nothing short of heroic. Back then, my French was limited to the few scraps salvaged from my school days. My attention in French class had been inversely proportional to the charisma of the teacher – except, of course, on those rare occasions when an attractive French assistant graced our all-boys school, suddenly making French the most fascinating subject on the planet.

Despite these educational shortcomings, with Jacques's guidance and a persistence that surprised even me, my French gradually evolved from a series of polite shrugs to actual sentences. It's safe to say that, over time, the language barrier became less of a problem.

Essentially the business model was the same as with all their acquisitions. We would look to reduce costs with significant workforce attrition while driving aggressive sales growth. In this case, the group had decided that such a business did not need seven hundred and fifty employees but could operate with at least forty percent less staff. This model may have worked in the UK, but this was France — where employment laws aren't just guidelines but more akin to sacred texts. The notion of making staff redundant with a mere pen stroke was as fantastical there as finding a Parisian street without a bakery.

Not only could we not arbitrarily fire people, but we were also obliged to either find them new jobs, retrain them, or pay exorbitant sums of money for them to be released from their contracts. Morally, this was brilliant, but commercially, it was a disaster. We had to employ an extra HR person, a lawyer and a recruitment consultant, and in the end, we carried the costs of the acquisition for two years instead of the original plan to sell the business in about twelve months.

My time with the conglomerate led to a significant wealth accumulation for its owners. I dedicated eight years, marked by high adrenaline and relentless pace, to the conglomerate's vision. While it served as a profound learning curve academically and in business acumen, its toll on my personal life was considerable. Following the sale of the French business and the departure of my mentor, the CEO, I found myself back in the boardroom of the UK parent company. The atmosphere, dominated by alpha personalities discussing the financial potential of their next acquisitions, was a familiar scene. At this point, I decided to leave, a decision that was neither easy nor immediate. This period marked not just the end of a millennium for me but also the beginning of a dramatic shift in both my business and personal life. Despite enduring a year of intense stress, high blood pressure, and long hours, my eventual departure from the conglomerate was accompanied by mixed emotions.

The earlier years in this testosterone-driven environment certainly had their highlights. Notably, I had the opportunity to work with one of the top minds in strategic planning, an ex-senior executive from a major global pharmaceutical corporation who also lectured at a premier UK business school. Under his mentorship for three years, I gained deep insights into theoretical knowledge and its practical application. Our interactions were intellectually stimulating. He was the only person I have ever met who could as easily converse in Latin, as English or French. However, aligning his theoretical expertise with practical business application was a continual challenge.

Resigning was not straightforward, especially as I

had no immediate job prospects. Yet, I remained convinced that my business recovery and growth skills could be applied more constructively elsewhere. Although unsure of my next step, I contemplated moving into the IT and technology sector. As the industry was emerging from its peak, I saw an opportunity to use my skills. It was a bitter-sweet parting, as there was much that I had learned and enjoyed in previous years in this macho, male-dominated, high-testosterone environment.

On the positive side:

- Adaptability in Diverse Business Environments. The experience of working across different countries, particularly in the dynamic setting of a multinational conglomerate, provided a valuable lesson for me in adaptability and the need to understand diverse business cultures.

- Importance of Team Dynamics. Working with a varied team, including a charismatic CEO, a highly pragmatic Operations Director, remarkably talented French teams and an influential mentor, highlighted the value of diverse perspectives and skills in a successful business operation.

- Effective Leadership and Mentorship. The opportunity to work under a significant mentor in strategic planning offered deep insights into theoretical knowledge and its practical application, emphasising the importance of good leadership and mentorship in professional growth.

- Resilience in High-Pressure Environments. The

high-adrenaline, fast-paced environment of the conglomerate taught me resilience and the ability to thrive under pressure.

- Market and Competitor Analysis Skills. The importance of working with skilled professionals, like the marketing and product management teams, adept in market and competitor research, enhanced skills in creating detailed sales playbooks and innovating new products.
- Language and Cultural Skills. The challenge of improving French language skills and adapting to a new culture was a significant personal and professional development. We Brits and Americans tend to think that everyone should speak our language.

Tempered by:

- Ethical and Moral Concerns in Business. The aggressive profit-driven strategies, including significant layoffs and cost-cutting measures, raised ethical concerns and questions about the sustainability and morality of such a business model.
- Challenges of International Business Laws. Encountering strict French employment laws contrasted sharply with the UK's more flexible laws, teaching the importance of understanding and respecting international business practices and legal frameworks.
- Personal Toll of Intense Work Environments. The

intense stress, long hours, and high-pressure environment of the conglomerate took a considerable personal toll, underscoring the importance of work-life balance.

- Challenges in Corporate Culture. The experience in a male-dominated, high-testosterone corporate environment highlighted the challenges and limitations of such a workplace culture that in modern business environments would not survive.
- Difficulty in Implementing Business Models Across Borders. The conglomerate's standard business model of rapid cost-cutting and workforce reduction faced practical and moral challenges when applied in France, showcasing the difficulty of implementing a one-size-fits-all approach in international business.

To elevate performance, you should evaluate and redesign your sales processes, emphasising the:

- Customer journey,
- Market dynamics and
- Sales team feedback.

Implementing a more adaptable and flexible sales process and additional training and support can revolutionise your sales approach. Regularly reviewing and updating these workflows is crucial to keep them relevant and effective. Remember, a sales process that adds value for customers encourages customers and the sales team to engage more fully.

Underperformance in this area might suggest that the sales processes are skewed towards the sales team's convenience rather than delivering value to customers.

Sales processes should be tailored according to the type of product, service, channel and relationship stage, from initial customer acquisition to nurturing strong relationships and cultivating customer advocates. To boost performance, reevaluate and redesign your sales processes with a customer-centric approach, understanding their needs, expectations and preferences at each relationship stage and tailoring the sales processes accordingly.

Prioritising customer value creation will better equip your sales team to establish meaningful connections, enhance customer satisfaction, and, ultimately, elevate sales performance.

Customer Winning

Securing customers is a synergistic effort, blending the strengths of sales and marketing teams. When done effectively, it can catalyse exponential growth for a company. High benchmark performance signifies that your company consistently scrutinises and enhances the:

- Content,
- Quality and
- Effectiveness

of its customer acquisition strategies, gauging success through sales results and customer feedback.

<u>The most successful organisations possess well-defined sales processes perfectly aligned with customer buying journeys.</u> Standardised methods for continuous improvement support them. These companies excel in understanding their customers' needs, preferences and pain points, enabling them to tailor their sales and marketing efforts for maximum impact. Moreover, they harness data-driven insights to refine their strategies and maintain a competitive edge in the market. Ensuring that sales processes and customer acquisition strategies are adaptable, customer-centric, and regularly tracked and measured is crucial for achieving exceptional and sustainable growth.

A lower quartile performance usually points to significant opportunities for improvement, as the effectiveness of sales activity is pivotal here. Winning new customers begins even before the sales team engages with prospects. Marketing activities must be aligned with the ideal target customer and timed perfectly to coincide with their buying cycle. Marketing and sales processes should be fully integrated, transcending the traditional view of marketing as just a lead generation and communication function.

The sales process can begin after identifying the ideal target customer, determining the best approach to attract them and mapping out their buying journey.

Recognisable key steps range from initial selection and prospect qualification to opportunity identification, possibly including a proof of concept or trial, proposal submission, negotiation and finally, deal closure. However, these steps alone don't guarantee proper customer alignment or provide enough detail for accurate tracking and management. The sales team should proactively anticipate the customer's likely next steps.

For each stage in the journey, the process should detail who is involved, the required actions and the timelines. If prospects require qualification, establish the procedure, timeline, and criteria. To qualify for an opportunity, a meeting with a predefined agenda, a qualification process and possibly a scoping document may be necessary. If the customer requests a proof of concept or trial, a clear policy and structured approach should be readily available.

The customer acquisition process should be mapped out to learn what works and what doesn't over time. For best practice, it should provide enough structure to measure where a new opportunity stands at any given time, with standardised methodologies and performance metrics offering a degree of predictability regarding deal closure likelihood. This approach streamlines the sales process and fosters continuous improvement and adaptation to changing customer needs and market dynamics.

Customer Onboarding

Exceptional customer engagement demands significant dedication in terms of communication and support. High performance reveals a company's commitment to continuously evaluating the quality and effectiveness of its customer onboarding processes, guided by consistent customer feedback. The most outstanding processes are those perfectly aligned with customer expectations and undergoing continuous refinement to meet evolving customer needs.

Beyond maintaining robust communication channels and offering prompt support, top-tier companies often provide comprehensive resources like tutorials, webinars and knowledge bases to guide customers through onboarding. This approach ensures that customers understand the product or service thoroughly and feel confident utilising it to its fullest potential. Assigning a dedicated customer success manager or team to each new customer can significantly elevate the onboarding experience, offering personalised guidance and tailored solutions for any challenges or concerns that may arise during the onboarding phase.

If your team is performing in the lower quartiles, it may indicate that key service elements are either missing or need enhancement. Winning a new customer is only part of the equation; many companies overlook the importance of effectively onboarding customers as a critical aspect of deal closure. When a business development team hands over a customer to internal account management or service teams post-deal, the customer may feel uncertain about their new point of contact or the next steps, leading to potential "buyer's remorse."

A meticulously planned handover process from field sales to internal account management is crucial to ensure seamless transitions. This process should involve a roadmap and briefing shared with the customer before and during the handover, clearly outlining communication channels, responsibilities and the roles of other organisational members who may impact them directly or indirectly. Ensuring the customer experiences a smooth transition from initial sales activities to the support and delivery provided by internal teams is paramount.

When the product or service requires involvement from multiple people, clarifying individual roles and responsibilities while assigning a single point of contact for the customer is vital. Like the customer acquisition process, each subsequent step in the customer journey should specify the involved parties, the tasks to be completed, and their deadlines.

Continual assessment and improvement of the onboarding process's quality and effectiveness are vital. Gathering and analysing customer feedback, not only during the onboarding process but also at regular intervals afterwards, allows companies to refine their processes, identify areas for improvement, and proactively address issues before they escalate. By consistently focusing on customer engagement, businesses can foster long-term relationships that ultimately lead to higher satisfaction and loyalty.

Customer Upselling

Acquiring new customers is merely the beginning of a journey that spirals into cultivating deep, enduring relationships and uncovering opportunities for enhanced engagement. Selling to existing customers is significantly more cost-effective than acquiring new ones, underscoring the vital need for your sales team and the entire organisation to excel in upselling.

High benchmark performance reflects a company's adeptness in effective account management, upselling, and consistently refining its account planning processes. These companies employ comprehensive multi-year account plans that are perfectly interwoven with broader business strategies. Achieving this level of expertise involves establishing clear communication channels with customers and proactively addressing their needs and concerns. This translates to regular check-ins, personalised offers and swift responses to inquiries. Moreover, effective account management is about nurturing long-term relationships, understanding customers' unique requirements, anticipating their future needs and staying attuned to market trends.

A customer-centric approach is the linchpin for success in upselling. Continually harvesting customer feedback enables organisations to pinpoint improvement areas and refine strategies that enhance the overall customer experience. Customised solutions, tailored support and exclusive benefits boost customer satisfaction and encourage loyalty that pave the way for increased sales and revenue growth.

Excelling in customer engagement and relationship management melds robust account planning with effective communication and a customer-focused mindset. Sharpening account management strategies fosters lasting customer relationships and unlocks the full potential of your existing customer base. Companies lagging in customer engagement and relationship management often have decreased customer satisfaction, higher churn rates, missed upselling opportunities, tarnished brand reputation and demoralised employees.

Upselling processes share similarities with customer acquisition but with an intensified focus on collaboration. If your team's benchmark performance is below average, examine the strength of relationships, opportunity matrices, account plans, and the upselling portion of the sales pipeline. Enhancing these areas can bolster your organisation's upselling capabilities and fortify customer relationships. Effective upselling begins with an in-depth understanding of the customer's business and identifying growth opportunities. When a customer's wallet share is maximised, and competitors are absent within the account, it's crucial to devise a strategy to safeguard, or "brick-wall", the account.

Craft detailed account plans that spotlight current and future opportunities, outlining their development strategies, responsible parties and timelines. This phase is critical for sustaining long-term customer retention and propelling business growth. Embracing technology solutions like CRM systems can streamline customer engagement processes, focusing efforts on building robust, enduring relationships. For customers, this relationship should feel like a collaborative partnership, with connections at multiple levels working jointly towards their goals.

Customer Retention and Renewal

Cultivating strong relationships with existing customers is a linchpin for fostering brand loyalty that translate into lifetime value and increased revenue over time. Companies excelling in this domain invest heavily in developing skills that are essential for maintaining and enhancing these relationships. A high benchmark performance indicates an organisation's prowess in an outstanding customer retention and renewal process continuously honed for excellence.

Such organisations ensure clear annual renewal visibility for all contracts and accounts, complemented by automated reminders set well ahead of renewal deadlines. This meticulous attention and organisation guarantee that customers are cognisant of upcoming renewals, providing ample opportunity to consider their options; thereby, nurturing trust and transparency.

To elevate customer retention and renewal, consider deploying personalised communication strategies, tailored service offerings, and regular check-ins to gauge customer satisfaction and proactively address concerns. If your team's performance is on the lower end in customer retention and renewals, it signals risks like revenue loss, decreased customer lifetime value and potential harm to your business reputation. Addressing this involves evaluating existing processes to pinpoint areas needing improvement. Enhancing customer communication builds trust and demonstrates your commitment. Automated reminders for contract renewals ensure no renewal opportunity is overlooked.

Tailoring solutions to meet unique customer needs can significantly boost satisfaction and loyalty. Regularly monitoring customer satisfaction through feedback allows for timely resolution of any issues. Additionally, investing in employee training and development programs equips your staff to engage more effectively with customers. Aligning incentives for sales and account management teams with customer retention and renewal goals fosters a culture prioritising long-term relationships.

Customer churn is inevitable despite best efforts, whether due to unawareness, contracts ending, or customers exploring alternatives. Even robust customer relationships can wane without diligent nurturing; complacency can creep in, often unnoticed until it's too late. Combat this by proactively identifying, understanding, and meticulously managing risk points in customer relationships. Incorporate regular performance reviews with key customers into sales processes and workflows alongside actionable plans for continuous product and service delivery improvement.

Clear processes, assigned responsibilities, and measurement plans are vital for businesses with long-term contracts. Ensure each account includes a series of pre-planned actions for sales and customer service teams to execute well before renewal deadlines.

Pillar 4: Organisation and Development

Several factors are instrumental in sculpting the organisation and its workforce. Paramount among these are:

- Attracting the right talent,
- Fostering a culture of continuous learning,
- Setting clear goals and expectations,
- Nurturing a positive work environment,
- Embodying effective leadership.

A well-defined organisational structure, infused with a strong, value-driven culture, streamlines communication, enhances decision-making processes and cultivates employees' unity and belonging.

Addressing these elements enables organisations to cultivate an environment where people flourish, leading to elevated performance, innovation and overarching success. If your company struggles in organisation and development, it's imperative to address the specific areas of concern strategically. Start by evaluating the existing organisational structure to ensure it facilitates efficient communication, decision-making and resource allocation. Identify and rectify bottlenecks, redundant roles and misalignments, considering a flatter hierarchy or cross-functional teams to encourage collaboration and agility.

Invest in robust employee training and development programs while defining clear, measurable, and achievable performance goals to align with the company's strategic objectives. Establish open and transparent communication within the organisation and promote a culture of constructive feedback and continuous improvement.

Employee engagement is essential thus, providing opportunities for growth, recognition, and participation in decision-making is key to maintaining motivation. Developing leadership skills in managers and executives equips them to lead, motivate, and manage their teams effectively.

Regular reviews, targeting improvement areas and measuring key performance indicators (KPIs) are crucial to track your organisation's and development initiatives' success.

Organisation and Structure

A high-performing organisation typically boasts a well-defined sales structure, with meticulously documented processes and clear role descriptions aligned with the business strategy and goals. As a company grows and seeks to expand or diversify its market share, re-evaluating the existing structure and systems, adjusting roles and proactively planning for anticipated growth becomes essential.

Maintaining an optimal sales organisation structure necessitates clear reporting lines and seamless communication channels between departments, fostering cross-functional collaboration. A continuous learning and improvement culture characterised by regular training sessions, workshops and coaching opportunities is a hallmark of high-performing organisations and structures. This empowers the sales team to adapt to changing market dynamics and stay abreast of industry trends.

Incorporating customer feedback and data-driven insights into the sales organisation's decision-making process ensures that the company remains customer-centric and agile. Establishing a robust performance management system to evaluate and reward employees based on their contributions and a merit-based incentive structure motivates the sales team to achieve their targets and nurtures a performance-driven culture.

A poorly structured sales organisation can face numerous challenges, impacting its overall performance and ability to achieve its goals. Resource allocation inefficiency can lead to wasted efforts, while unclear roles and responsibilities can cause confusion and reduced accountability among team members. Poor communication and collaboration can result in disjointed strategies and a subpar customer experience.

Recruitment and Selection

The hallmark of a high-performing organisation is a workforce that is motivated, focused and well-trained, complemented by fair compensation and recognition for their contributions. The organisation's commitment to nurturing its workforce through comprehensive recruitment and selection processes is at the heart of this success. Organisations should prioritise clear communication and transparency in their hiring practices, offering candidates a positive experience. Objective assessments of skills, experience, and cultural fit should be utilised, such as structured interviews and relevant evaluations. By treating all applicants professionally, organisations can maintain a positive reputation and leave a lasting impression.

To truly excel in this area, organisations must create an environment that values continuous learning, offering employees opportunities for professional growth through training and development initiatives. A collaborative and inclusive work culture, valuing diversity and different perspectives, will foster a sense of trust and shared purpose.

Competitive compensation and benefits packages should be implemented, reflecting the value employees bring to the organisation. Promoting work-life balance and providing resources to help employees manage personal and professional responsibilities is essential. Celebrating individual and collective successes further strengthens the workforce's commitment and engagement.

If your team's performance is on the lower end in recruitment and selection, it is crucial to examine your process and align it with best practices. Effective recruitment and selection depend on various factors, such as:

- Resources,
- Organisational size,
- Structure and
- Vision.

These elements determine the nature of the roles within the organisation and the types of candidates best suited for those positions. Efficient hiring processes can significantly impact the speed of induction and sales achievement.

Start by defining the role specification based on the expected outcomes. For instance, if the goal is to acquire new customers, hiring a salesperson with relevant skills and experience would be sensible rather than someone better suited for managing major accounts. Similarly, managing channel partners necessitates specific expertise beyond typical sales roles. When the job description is well-defined, and the search begins, implement a process that validates candidates' experience, assesses their knowledge and skills, and evaluates their alignment with your organisation's values. Designing key questions based on the job specification, values, knowledge, and skills, alongside a scoring mechanism, will streamline and improve the process for all parties involved.

Before recruiting a new salesperson, create a comprehensive induction plan outlining clear objectives and a schedule for the first thirty/sixty/ninety days. This plan should include testing and training to ensure the new employee comprehends the required knowledge and can apply it to customer engagement. Although this may seem overly detailed for some organisations, a well-executed induction plan builds the recruit's confidence and helps them achieve their goals more effectively.

Align recruitment and retention programs to attract high-calibre candidates and offer opportunities for development and growth within your organisation. By focusing on these aspects, your organisation will benefit from a more engaged, skilled workforce committed to achieving success.

Competency Management

In high-performing organisations, ongoing performance management and development are not just initiatives — they're integral to the fabric of the business. Such organisations are made up of high-performing individuals driven by efficient processes that continually evaluate and nurture knowledge and skills across the board. To build a thriving and adaptable workforce, the focus should be on honing general and sales-specific skills.

General skills — like leadership, communication, problem-solving, and teamwork — lay the groundwork for success in any role. Sales-specific skills, such as negotiation, lead generation, and customer relationship management, are vital in driving business growth and maintaining a competitive edge. Investing in employee development through continuous training, mentorship, and skill-building opportunities is pivotal. This approach hones the workforce's capabilities and boosts engagement, satisfaction, and retention, attracting top talent and creating a resilient, agile team.

If your company lags in performance management and employee development, the ripple effects can be significant, touching every aspect of business health and success. Employees may become disengaged and less productive, leading to high turnover rates. The company might also struggle to attract and retain top talent which is a key driver of growth and innovation.

Skills and knowledge can stagnate if not consistently refreshed, leaving the workforce ill-equipped to meet evolving business demands. This can erode your organisation's competitive stance, stifle its innovation capacity, and hinder its adaptability to market changes and opportunities.

Clearly defined goals and achievement plans are necessary for a sales organisation poised for growth. These should be supported by well-structured sales processes, as previously discussed. However, the most impactful factor on business performance is the sales team members' quality of sales knowledge, skills and activities.

The journey to success begins with pinpointing the specific knowledge, skills and activities needed for the sales team to hit its targets. This encompasses a broad spectrum of knowledge areas – from products and services to pricing, customers, ideal target prospects, company information and key competitors. Additionally, many sales skills are required, including:

- Prospecting,
- Winning and onboarding customers,
- Managing meetings and presentations,
- Account management and upselling,
- Negotiation and
- Personal development.

Understanding, applying and measuring these skills effectively, both individually and collectively, is critical. Recognise that not every salesperson will be a superstar from the start. Focus on developing and coaching individual competencies within local teams or across different regions. This involves creating sales-focused competency models linked to personal development plans and training programs.

While developing these models and plans may demand time and effort, the investment pays dividends in the long run. By consistently nurturing each team member's competencies and providing tailored training and development opportunities, a sales organisation can build a highly skilled and efficient workforce, driving sustainable growth and success.

Talent Management

Organisations that stand out in talent management and development, often found in the upper echelons, engage in continuous improvement processes and reviews. These processes, bolstered by a strong executive focus on sales and clearly defined leadership progression pathways, position the organisation to retain and grow its top talent. Understanding the aspirations of high-performing employees and creating opportunities that align with these ambitions while ensuring business viability elevates a company from good to great.

Regular performance reviews and development discussions with employees are essential, providing valuable feedback and identifying areas for improvement. Setting realistic goals that resonate with the employee's aspirations and the organisation's strategic objectives is key. Access to training programs, mentorship, and cross-functional projects helps employees build on their strengths and address weaknesses, contributing to their professional development.

Fostering a culture of open communication and transparency encourages employees to share their career goals, facilitating a collaborative approach to talent development. This helps organisations tailor career paths that meet employee expectations and align with the company's long-term goals and vision.

Investing in talent management and development:

- Creates a more engaged and motivated workforce,
- Reduces turnover,
- Maximises company and employee potential.

The repercussions can be profound when a company underperforms in talent management and development. High turnover rates can become a significant issue, as employee dissatisfaction leads to departures, increasing recruitment and training costs and causing operational disruptions. Employee engagement may suffer, impacting productivity, innovation and overall company performance.

Attracting top talent becomes challenging for companies that don't prioritise talent development, as skilled professionals often seek growth opportunities and supportive work environments. Without proper strategies, a company might fail to fully leverage its employees' skills and potential, leading to underperformance and missed growth opportunities.

Retaining and nurturing talented individuals, whether new recruits or outstanding performers already on your team, is crucial for maintaining high motivation, satisfaction and performance levels. Developing a deep understanding of each individual's unique motivators and aspirations is essential. Psychometric assessments can provide insights into personal traits, preferences and communication styles, enhancing self-awareness and improving workplace dynamics.

For employees on a fast-track promotion path, establishing clear goals and milestones they genuinely believe in is vital. Collaborate with them to develop comprehensive learning and development plans, outlining required training or coaching, responsible parties for delivery, timelines, and success criteria.

Outstanding performance must be rewarded through:

- Tangible incentives,
- Recognition and
- Affirmation.

Ensure that the entire team perceives that reward schemes are transparent, easily understood and fair. Additionally, carefully consider whether the incentives used effectively drive the desired outcomes.

Organisations lacking a structured approach to talent management, minimal executive recognition of sales talent, unclear leadership progression paths, or ineffective reward structures may experience demotivated and less productive team members. This decline in motivation and productivity can negatively impact sales performance and, ultimately, the company's bottom line.

Personal Development

In high-performing organisations, employee personal development planning is beneficial and a cornerstone for both employer and employee growth. Scoring in the upper quartiles of the survey signifies an organisation's mastery in implementing robust systems and processes to pinpoint and foster each team member's growth potential. Performance improvement commences with a thorough assessment of the knowledge and skills individuals need to excel in their roles. Establishing key performance criteria and KPIs paves the way for evaluating individual performance against these benchmarks.

This methodology emphasises recognising each individual's strengths and weaknesses, opening doors for feedback, mentoring and growth. Experience suggests that such a process cultivates a profound sense of ownership and value among employees and the team. Tailoring personalised learning and development plans that are regularly measured and monitored can bolster the entire team. Recognising that people learn differently and at varying paces is pivotal for achieving peak performance across a team or an entire organisation.

Investing in personal development planning fosters a culture of continuous improvement, empowering employees to realise their full potential. This not only amplifies productivity but also nurtures employee satisfaction and loyalty.

A company struggling in personal development planning may face challenges such as decreased employee morale and motivation, higher turnover rates, skill and knowledge gaps, reduced competitiveness and stifled innovation. When employees sense a lack of attention to their growth, disengagement ensues, leading to diminished productivity and job satisfaction and increased attrition.

Stagnant skills and knowledge hinder the workforce's ability to meet evolving business demands, weakening the organisation's competitive stance. A workforce not encouraged to grow may contribute less in terms of new ideas or solutions, limiting the organisation's capacity for innovation and adaptation. To redress these issues, prioritise creating and implementing individualised personal development plans. This involves assessing each employee's strengths, weaknesses and development needs;

establishing performance criteria and KPIs; designing tailored learning and development plans; providing continuous feedback, mentoring, and growth opportunities and ensuring management and leadership support employee development.

Personal development plans should encompass more than just sales figures; they should include non-financial goals and learning objectives. When employees feel valued and recognised, teamwork thrives, leading to extraordinary performance, heightened sales revenue and profit, and customer satisfaction.

Without structured personal development planning, team cohesion suffers, adversely impacting sales growth. The personal planning process must be adaptable to individual employees, the team, and business changes and regularly reviewed for quality and effectiveness. Engage team members in dialogue about crucial knowledge, skills, and qualifications needed in their market. Foster open communication, promote on-the-job coaching and mentoring, and routinely analyse performance against defined criteria to enhance knowledge, skills, and execution.

Remuneration

In compensation management, best practices encompass a policy that aligns with both company and individual goals, successfully linking performance achievement, personal development, and rewards.

Compensation levels and market demands can differ widely across countries and industries. In competitive markets, effectively aligning performance, development, and rewards is crucial for attracting top talent and realising organisational goals. The allure and retention of exceptional performers often hinge on the competitiveness of compensation and benefits packages.

Top-tier companies routinely evaluate and update their compensation strategies to remain relevant and competitive. Factors to consider include industry benchmarks, cost-of-living adjustments, and shifting market conditions. Moreover, crafting a comprehensive compensation package that extends beyond monetary rewards to non-financial incentives, such as career development opportunities, flexible working arrangements, and a positive work environment, is imperative.

When a company falls short in compensation management, it faces several far-reaching challenges. Struggling to attract top talent is a primary concern, as skilled candidates may opt for competitors with more attractive compensation packages. Inadequate compensation can lead to:

- Employee dissatisfaction,
- Increased turnover and
- Associated costs.

Motivation and engagement may wane if employees perceive their rewards as misaligned with their skills, efforts and contributions. This can result in diminished productivity and overall performance. Moreover, an unfair or non-competitive compensation system can breed resentment and tension among team members that in turn negatively impacts company culture and teamwork. If high-performing employees feel underappreciated, they might seek opportunities elsewhere.

While financial remuneration is not always the primary motivator, inadequate compensation can significantly demotivate team members. Issues like unequal pay packages, lack of incentives, and shifting goalposts in reward schemes contribute to dissatisfaction. The true motivators often include deal closure, customer wins, and recognition from peers and clients. However, money becomes a demotivating factor if compensation is considered insufficient or sales targets unattainable.

Compensation schemes should be straightforward, offering sufficient incentives to promote desired outcomes. These schemes must be financially sensible and not overly complex for both employers and employees. Besides revenue or profit growth, other key performance factors, such as customer satisfaction or product and service mix, should be considered in the remuneration strategy.

For employees performing equivalent roles, compensation schemes should be equitable. While factors like length of service, experience, or exceptional performance might justify higher base salaries for some, the overall compensation structure must be perceived as fair across the board.

Culture and Communications

Effective internal and external communication and aligning perception with reality are hallmarks of high-performing organisations. These organisations champion positive, supportive, transparent values and culture, maintaining clear communication processes.

<u>Establishing a value-driven, supportive culture should be a priority for any organisation. A culture that promotes employee well-being and satisfaction has a direct, positive impact on performance.</u> When employees thrive in a positive work environment, they are happier, more motivated and more likely to deliver their best, resulting in superior outcomes.

Organisations should emphasise open and honest communication internally among team members and externally with customers, partners and stakeholders to cultivate such a culture. Encourage collaboration, teamwork and the sharing of ideas, recognising that diversity of thought can drive innovation and improved performance. Prioritise employee development, offering opportunities for growth and skill-building, regular feedback and performance evaluations. This supports individual progress and reinforces the organisation's commitment to its employees' success.

Leaders should exemplify the organisation's values,

setting a standard for employees to emulate. When employees see their leaders genuinely upholding the company's principles, they are more likely to feel aligned with and committed to the organisation's mission and vision. Organisations can enhance employee satisfaction, performance, and overall success by fostering a value-driven, supportive culture and prioritising clear communication.

If your company performs poorly in internal and external communication or cultivating a positive, supportive, and value-driven culture, it may face various challenges that can hinder overall success. Employees in such an environment may experience low morale, decreased job satisfaction and reduced engagement, leading to lower productivity and performance. Furthermore, high employee turnover could become a significant issue as disenchanted employees seek more fulfilling opportunities elsewhere, increasing recruitment costs and losing valuable talent.

Effective communication is crucial in creating a high-performing environment and shaping how clients and stakeholders perceive your organisation in the marketplace. Good communication is achieved when all parties involved reach a common understanding. Company culture, a set of shared values within the business, may not always be overtly evident, but articulating these values is essential for employees, suppliers, and customers to understand and embrace.

When interacting with customers, vendors, or

business partners, it is vital to understand how their business values and cultures align with yours. For organisations involved in international business, comprehending diverse cultural norms is crucial to establishing effective communication strategies. Approaches that are successful in one region may not be appropriate in another, as cultural differences can significantly influence business practices.

Regardless of your company's size, the potential for miscommunication is ever-present. A poorly worded email can greatly impact the recipient's interpretation, and humour perceived in one culture might be completely misunderstood in another. To address these challenges, having a well-thought-out and implemented sales playbook that guides communication across various scenarios is essential. This includes crafting careful emails, applying universal guidelines, designing sales pitches that consider the cultural and business practices of the target audience, in addition to addressing commercial and technical propositions.

Robust internal communication processes and solid business values ensure employees understand and embody the organisation's shared values, goals and aspirations. In doing so, they can communicate these values to the external world positively and engagingly, enhancing your brand reputation and fostering a supportive, high-performing work environment.

Case Study: More than a Money-Making Machine

The company was very special and unique.

Following initial successes, I transitioned to a larger UK-based manufacturing company with approximately 10,000 employees. This new challenge also bore the hallmarks of a turnaround story. But it was a team effort with an eight-member core team at the forefront of this transformation. Despite being relatively young in my thirties, this period was instrumental for my understanding of business transformation.

It was a QUANGO (a shortening of "quasi NGO" – a non-government organisation). Established in 1946 as an integral part of the Employment Services' Sheltered Employment Programme, its mission was to provide productive employment and training within sheltered conditions for people with severe disabilities who could work. They had businesses in engineering, technology, furniture manufacturing and across a spectrum of other sectors, with about ninety-five factories.

It was to become, for me, one of the most inspiring business environments on a professional and personal level.

However, this was in Margaret Thatcher's time as Prime Minister, whose mission was to make public sector enterprises more commercial and self-sufficient. We were all brought into this business with the ultimate goal of reversing the funding so that the government share was reduced from seventy-five per cent to twenty-five per cent.

Because of the nature of employment, they had approximately four times more employees than in a traditional business. Capital investment in manufacturing plants and equipment was high, focusing on low-cost, high-volume manufacturing with repeat purchasing and standard product lines. They had a concept called "factory loading", which meant the factories needed to keep up volumes irrespective of sales margins.

The challenge was that the nature of the workforce meant that people were trained to carry out certain operations and if demand fell for that particular kind of product, the labour force had to be retrained for another operation, which created a lot of idle time and cost. This led to an absolute focus on finding volume orders at all costs, irrespective of profit margins. Over the years, some distributors and customers have taken advantage of this, driving prices down, often to the point where products were sold at a significant loss.

The contract furniture division had four hundred and thirty eight disabled and sixty-seven fit employees, with a head office and four out of ninety-five group manufacturing facilities. They traditionally supplied tables, desks, chairs and stools for the UK educational furniture market.

However, legislative changes in the educational

sector, slow growth in the UK economy and political developments within Europe brought about a challenging period of change.

In the UK, educational legislation changed the nature of schools management and buying, creating a fragmentation of the buying system with approximately one hundred and twenty traditional buying points expanding to twenty-seven thousand. This led to a consequent shift in distribution channel approach, undisciplined pricing, increased competition and increased customer choice and demand for quality, availability and service. The net effect had been an industry shortfall in orders of fifteen percent below the previous year. So, although the nature of this business was different, it also became a turnaround story.

There were several advantages over other businesses. Although the workforce was larger, it was full of motivated people working with highly evolved operational processes, including high-quality product design, manufacturing, delivery and customer support.

The real challenges were selling in a highly competitive and changing market, government requirements for cost reduction and profit growth and significantly undervalued product pricing, with customers benefiting from years of prices on an average of twenty-five percent lower than commercial market rates.

The key drivers of success included:

Strategic and Detailed Operational Planning

We called it "The EGMAP" or Ever Green Moving Action Plan. This involved creating a five-year planning horizon with very detailed road map planning and measurement in year one, with less detail in year two and so on through to year five. In the second year, year two in the original plan became year one. Although plans changed along the way, they focused on precisely which market sectors we could capture, what the business was trying to achieve and how we planned to bring it about.

With almost eighty-six thousand product SKUs, we could still achieve a ninety-five per cent or more accuracy in the forecast to actual manufacturing volumes on a twelve-month horizon through careful planning and tight sales pipeline processes and management.

Building a Market-Leading Brand

In what had become a highly competitive marketplace, we had a significant strength and reputation for delivering high-quality products, but with a Public Sector image as a company that could be exploited for low prices. We therefore created a whole new range of products and a modern-looking brand, underpinned by the group's strength for quality and reliability of manufacture. Every opportunity was used to communicate this brand into the market in a way that dominated our competition. We became well-known for our creative and sometimes outrageous marketing campaigns. One example, when exhibiting at large events in the UK and Switzerland, involved employing a team of actors to write and enact a play about how our products were typically used in a customer environment. Additionally, they created colourful "living statues" on all the main routes from the airports and rail stations into the exhibition halls. It was so successful, that our competitors complained to the organisers that we were making too much of a presence. It was quite remarkable, great fun and highly successful.

Confidence in Our Pricing Strategy

This was probably the toughest thing to achieve with a history of selling quality products well below market value through channel partners who were used to making considerably more margin than us as the manufacturer. Essentially we needed a price increase of at least twenty-five per cent. The biggest hurdle initially was an internal one. The management was extremely cautious for fear of losing factory loading and the sales teams disagreed, fearing they would lose customers overnight. In practice, a few channel partners were difficult to persuade but eventually agreed to a phasing and compromise.

LEAN Business Principles

In the days of TQM and LEAN in manufacturing, we realised that a similar approach could be taken amongst the sales and marketing teams. Initially, it was a challenge but eventually a resounding success as it gave us structure and measurability that made sales and forecasting much more predictable.

Ultimately, we achieved our goals successfully, delivering forty-eight per cent revenue growth within three years and reducing the government investment to below twenty-five per cent with the balance from commercial margins.

Pillar 5: Knowledge and Skill

In high-performing sales teams, knowledge and skill development are paramount. This focus transcends basic planning and procedural adherence, positioning the depth of expertise and its strategic application as the primary drivers of exceptional sales results. For sales teams to thrive and outperform, it's essential to identify which areas of knowledge are crucial and how these can be developed and effectively applied. While robust planning and structured processes provide a solid foundation, the real catalyst for standout sales achievements lies in the depth and application of the team's knowledge and skills. As every failed super team in professional sports history can tell you, it's great to put all the pieces together of guys who have dominated the league individually, but if they can't work together on the court, the pitch, or the field, it's just a waste of everyone's time.

As the head coach of the England football team, speaking at one of our sales conferences, told us,

"Each player is a diamond in their own right, but diamonds can have sharp edges, and the challenge is getting them aligned perfectly together." Continuous investment in tailored training and development is key. This approach should encompass an evaluation of individual and collective strengths, areas requiring growth and providing diverse educational resources. It's about nurturing an environment where continuous learning is encouraged and integrated into the team's ethos.

Encouraging a culture where knowledge is shared, experiences are exchanged, and best practices are discussed, elevates team performance. Such a collaborative environment boosts morale and fosters a sense of collective purpose and achievement. The impact can be significant when sales teams are not adequately equipped with the necessary knowledge and skills. For example, a lack of comprehensive understanding of the product range or the inability to align products with customer needs can severely limit the team's capacity to secure business. Similarly, shortcomings in essential sales skills – such as customer prospecting, effective questioning, or applying proven sales methodologies – can lead to declining performance levels. For sales professionals aiming to excel, embracing a cycle of continuous learning, improvement, and practical application is crucial. Sharing insights about what strategies work (or don't) with customers across different regions, can raise the bar for the entire sales organisation.

Developing a system that collectively addresses knowledge and skill factors for each salesperson and the team is essential for consistent growth. Implementing a continuous learning and development programme tailored to individual and team needs lays a foundational benchmark for high performance. Regularly assessing knowledge and skills in light of experience ensures the sales team remains dynamic and adaptable.

Key drivers of sales performance, such as activity volume, value, direction, knowledge, and skill, must be aligned and focused to achieve desired outcomes. Sales professionals must understand how to effectively communicate their company's value proposition and possess the necessary skills to engage customers and convert opportunities into successful sales. In businesses, these drivers are within the control of the sales function. The focused and skilled application of knowledge and activity determines success. Missing or poorly applied elements can derail goals, emphasising the importance of comprehensive understanding and skilful execution.

The heart of driving and delivering extraordinary performance lies in motivated people, whose confidence and motivation stem from their depth of knowledge and skill. A well-trained salesperson, comfortable and knowledgeable about their offerings, is more likely to engage with customers and achieve positive outcomes confidently. This type of professional is often on point because they are being paid to perform a duty that they excel at and enjoy. In sales, a lot of that is natural instinct; clearly, some people were born to talk a lot and convince others to their positions, but when you combine that talent with impressive training and positioning, you're creating a much more powerful individual.

To make a second sports analogy in a very small amount of space, a coach once told me that with athletes, there were three types of success. The first athlete succeeds because of their God-given talents; they were naturally born to be able to run faster, jump higher and endure harsh conditions or elements for longer periods. The second athlete succeeds by outworking the competition. They might not be the strongest or the fastest, but their willpower allows them to close those gaps rapidly based on effort and desire to prove themselves. The third type of athlete who succeeds has the natural ability and combines it with being the hardest worker out there. It is a very rare thing, but when you combine the two, that athlete – and, for our purposes, that salesperson – is a force of nature. Empowering your sales staff with the most knowledge in the field at their fingertips allows you to create super-sales people.

Diverse training methods, including classroom sessions and practical workshops, should be complemented by skill-building exercises relevant to the sales role. Recognising that individuals in a sales team have different learning styles is critical; hence, a one-size-fits-all approach to training is insufficient for holistic performance improvement.

The starting point for any high-performing sales team is an accurate assessment of each team member's current knowledge, skills and experience. Key considerations include understanding which factors are crucial in specific business or customer scenarios and ensuring the right people with the right aptitude are in the right roles. Once a clear understanding of the team's capabilities is established, developing a focused and effective training and development plan becomes feasible. This plan should target the most impactful areas for growth, tailored to individual and team needs. Nurturing high-performing sales teams requires a deep understanding of the necessary knowledge and skills and a commitment to continuously refine and direct these elements towards achieving successful outcomes. The right blend of knowledge, skill and focused activity, tailored to individual and team strengths, is the formula for building and sustaining high-performing sales teams and businesses. While meticulous planning, well-structured processes and KPIs lay the groundwork, the real driving force behind exceptional sales performance is the depth of your team's knowledge and skill in effectively wielding that knowledge.

Investing in ongoing training and development tailored to your team's unique needs is pivotal. This might entail evaluating individual strengths, weaknesses and growth areas; providing resources and opportunities for learning through workshops, seminars and online courses; and nurturing a supportive environment that champions continuous learning and improvement. Promoting a culture of collaboration and knowledge-sharing within the team can significantly elevate overall performance. Encouraging team members to exchange insights, experiences and best practices can lift cohesion and motivation. Below-par performance can adversely affect the length, quality and efficacy of your sales pipeline performance and closure rates. For instance, if the team lacks a thorough understanding of the product portfolio or fails to align it with customer needs effectively, their business-winning capability is compromised.

Lacking the skills to prospect new customers effectively, employ discovery questioning techniques, or apply a proven sales methodology to overcome objections consistently will inevitably lead to underperformance. Similarly, if marketing, direct, or channel sales teams miss the mark in identifying and targeting "ideal" customers with a fitting proposition, they risk squandering valuable time and forgoing potential sales. This entails an ongoing learning, improvement and application cycle for top-performing sales professionals. It's vital that they share with customers their knowledge about strategies that work or don't. If your teams are distributed across multiple regions, encourage cross-border learning and sharing of successes and failures to uplift the entire sales organisation.

To foster consistent growth and development, implement a system that collectively addresses each salesperson and team's knowledge and skill factors. A knowledge and skills programme of continuous learning and embracing individual and team development creates an essential and structured basis for high-performing teams. It provides a benchmark for personal development planning, coaching and activity-based learning. Within this, it is best practice to have regular knowledge and skills assessments in light of experience every six months between managers and their team members. These sessions should normally last two to three hours, with an agenda to go through goals, aspirations, areas for potential growth as well as where help is needed.

Naturally, there are many factors that influence performance, some outside the direct control of the salesperson or marketing team, such as products or services aligned to customer needs, a value proposition differentiated from the competition, or the resources, support and customer service excellence needed to delight customers. However, key sales performance drivers are within the direct control of the sales function; unless these are properly aligned and there is a clear understanding of what needs to be done and when then goals can fall short or be missed altogether.

As we see on the chart below, the key elements that will drive performance in achieving goals, whether they are financial or non-financial sales targets, on the one side are related to the volume, value, and direction of activity. Critically, on the other axis, we have knowledge and skill.

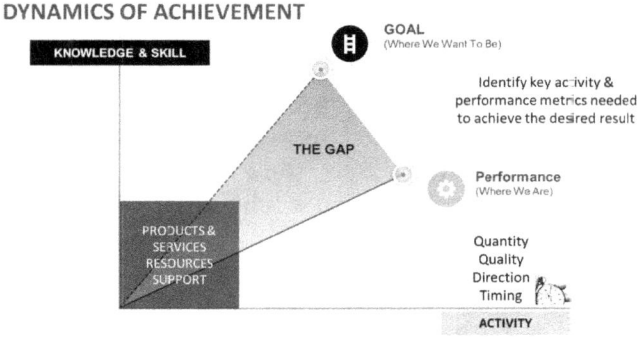

If a salesperson does not understand how to articulate what the company sells or does not have the skills to develop customer problems into needs and commitment to action, sales performance and goal achievement will be impaired. It is about understanding the customer situation and how your products or services can help. The salesperson needs the skills to manage the situation and engage with the customer at their level: making great calls, knowing what to ask and when, handling objections before they arise, and much more. In all businesses, these are performance drivers within the salesperson's control. Their knowledge, skill and activity focused on going in the right direction at the right time, and so on, determines the outcome. If any of those things are missing or poorly applied, the goal will fall short and not be achieved. It's important to understand what all these elements are and how to apply them. This will significantly improve the chances of a positive outcome.

Planning is everything and processes are critical in keeping the business on track, but motivated people are the key to driving and delivering extraordinary performance. What makes people confident and motivated is their depth of knowledge and skill. If a salesperson knows what they are talking about and has reasonable sales skills, they will feel happy and comfortable talking with the customer. If they are uncertain, afraid the customer might ask something they do not know, they will not perform as well, have a less engaged prospect and potentially lose the sale. A sales team could engage in classroom training programs, maybe on account management, process mapping or making great calls, but it will soon be lost unless they have the skills needed for the role and the salesperson knows how to apply that learning in practice.

Importantly, individuals in a sales team will have

different learning abilities, so giving everyone standardised classroom training or asking them to read a book or sit at the computer screen and watch "expert" videos will only partly deliver what is needed for performance improvement. The starting point must be knowing the current state of the union in terms of knowledge, skills, and experience for each individual and then the team as a whole. Which factors are more important than others in each business or customer situation? What personalities make up the sales team? Are the right people in the right jobs and have they got the skills and aptitude to do what is being asked of them? Trying to put a square peg into a round hole will not work. The right people need to be chosen to do the job they are being asked to do and then provided with the knowledge and the skills training to do it.

Once a baseline has been established, creating a development plan at an individual, team and company level is possible – focusing on what matters most. To grow people and the businesses they are operating in, it is necessary to develop a deep understanding of what knowledge and skills are needed and how these can be improved and focused to achieve the desired result. It is equally important to ensure that in selecting the salespeople and team, they have the right experience and aptitude for the job they are being asked to perform.

Case Study: Recruit Slowly and Fire Fast

One of the greatest examples of best practices coming out of the global sustainability company was its approach to delivering highly effective recruitment and induction. Recruitment is a critical aspect of building a successful organisation. The consequences of having the wrong people in key roles can be significant, hindering progress and performance.

The first step in a sound recruitment process is acknowledging our inherent biases. Everyone has them and they can unknowingly influence hiring decisions. Especially in small companies, it's important to involve others in the recruitment process to ensure a variety of perspectives and a more objective approach. Central to recruitment is the precise definition of the role. This involves understanding the position's responsibilities and identifying the essential skills and qualities required. These are the critical factors, or "big rocks", that a candidate must possess. Such clarity guides the recruitment process and sets clear expectations for the role.

The inundation of CVs in the digital age poses a challenge. The key is to focus on the essential qualities identified earlier and screen candidates against these criteria. This process requires a balance of objectivity and discernment. Interviews are where a candidate's true capabilities often emerge. For example, a common approach in sales positions is a two-stage interview. The first stage might be a presentation where candidates must demonstrate their understanding of the company and ability to communicate effectively. This reveals much about their preparation and presentation skills. Interviews are also where many great resumes are revealed as utter fabrications. Never be afraid to ask questions about a specific point on someone's resume to see if they really know what they are talking about. People of all ages, education levels, and experience strata are guilty of overstating who they are and what they're capable of when there's a job on the line.

The most telling sign of a candidate's potential is their initiative to go beyond the readily available information. Those who proactively engage with employees and conduct independent research show a level of dedication and insight that is highly valuable. The final stage often involves a practical, scenario-based challenge simulating real-world situations. This tests their technical and analytical skills, adaptability and problem-solving abilities – an example from my experience involved asking candidates to plan a market expansion in Europe. The most impressive candidates were those who supplemented the provided data with their research and presented well-considered strategies.

Even when mistakes are made, such as incorrect data in a presentation, a candidate's response to the error can be very telling. How they handle the situation can reveal qualities like resilience and adaptability, which are invaluable in business. Equally, the context of local employment laws plays a crucial role, especially in regions like Southern

Europe where the legal landscape is markedly different from places like the United States or the United Kingdom. In these areas, hiring someone can almost equate to a lifelong commitment. The difficulty in terminating employment makes the recruitment decision all the more critical. A case in point happened once when I was working in France. I was involved with a client who faced a challenging situation following the recruitment of a sales manager. The candidate seemed impeccable on paper – a strong CV and positive references and the company's recruitment process, seemingly thorough, led to his hiring. However, the reality of his performance quickly diverged from expectations. The initial month, filled with standard inductions, gave way to concerning signs in the following two months. This sales manager consistently failed to meet targets and engage effectively. The problem was brought to the CEO's attention, stressing the urgency given the probationary period governed by local employment laws. However, despite these warnings, the CEO extended the manager's probation, confident in his eventual improvement. This decision proved costly. The three-month probationary period is critical under southern European labour laws, particularly in France. Extending beyond this without addressing performance issues can lead to complicated and expensive termination processes. Five months later, the CEO acknowledged the problem, but by then, the financial implications of terminating the sales manager were severe – a staggering cost of 260,000 euros. This incident was not just a financial burden; it also represented lost opportunities and revenue.

This example is a cautionary tale about the importance of rigorous recruitment processes, particularly in regions with stringent employment laws. It emphasises the need for a recruitment strategy that goes beyond the surface level of CVs and references, incorporating a comprehensive understanding of a candidate's true potential and whether or not they are fit for the role. Moreover, it highlights the necessity of adhering to probationary periods and addressing performance issues promptly to avoid costly consequences.

Once the recruitment process ends with selecting a candidate, the next pivotal step is induction. This phase is critical in determining their success or failure in the company. It is here that many organisations get it wrong, leading to early disengagement, underperformance and, in the worst-case scenario, the loss of employment.

A poorly thought-through induction can look like this: The new hire is introduced to the CEO, who imparts the company's vision and strategy in a brief meeting. Following this, they meet with various team leaders, such as the Head of Production, each providing an overview of their department. Often, this process involves the new employee spending significant time just listening to presentations. This approach, while informative, can be passive and disengaging. I've experienced this firsthand when joining a client for an induction. I was primarily in a passive listening role for six weeks, attending presentations without active involvement. This method was ineffective — by the end of this period, I wasn't equipped to perform the tasks I had been shown simply because I hadn't been actively engaged in the learning process.

The ideal induction should be dynamic and interactive, especially for sales roles. These individuals, often high achievers, thrive on engagement and challenge. Keeping them in a passive role, even briefly, can lead to frustration and a sense of underutilisation. The answer lies in a structured thirty/sixty/ninety day induction program. This programme should be interactive, involving the new hire in learning. For example, after spending time with the product manager learning about the product line, the new salesperson should present this information to the management team or relevant group. This active involvement reinforces their learning and prepares them for client interactions. The core idea is to transition the new employee from a passive listener to an active participant. By the time they face the customer, they should be able to represent the company and its products as confidently and effectively as you would.

This method seems straightforward, yet many companies overlook its importance. A well-designed induction programme is not just about information dissemination but integration, engagement and empowerment. By investing in such a process, companies can significantly enhance their new hires' productivity and job satisfaction, ensuring a quicker and more effective integration into their roles.

Managing Relationships

In high-performing organisations, the art of managing relationships, both internally and externally, is pivotal in influencing the quantity and quality of communications, significantly impacting overall business performance. These organisations exhibit robust communication practices, continuously refined and improved, embodying core values and a culture focused on delivering customer excellence at every level. The key to managing relationships is empowering customer-focused teams with the necessary skills, time and resources to deepen collaborative efforts, nurturing existing relationships while consistently creating new ones. This nvolves systematic feedback loops and frequent performance reviews to ensure customers receive personalised support and prioritised investment in critical relationships. A culture that emphasises open communication, collaboration and continuous improvement not only strengthens internal dynamics but also enhances the external reputation of these organisations.

Managing relationships can face challenges, such as disagreements, role changes, supplier policy shifts, or competitors encroaching on market share. These issues, particularly among major accounts or prospective clients, call for a close examination of account relationship mapping to identify potential strengths and weaknesses. Much like in our personal and romantic lives, relationships demand dedicated effort, time and prioritisation. In sales, understanding the direct relationship with key customer contacts, the entire buying team and a broader group of stakeholders is crucial. This understanding significantly impacts nurturing sales opportunities, pipeline conversion, account management, and customer advocacy.

If your business struggles with client conversion or retention, reassess your sales team's capability in establishing and maintaining client relationships. A low performance in this area should prompt you to ask:

- Are all customers receiving personalised support?
- Are critical relationships being prioritised?
- Do the sales team possess the necessary skills in networking and relationship-building?

The advent of video conferencing and online communications has added complexity. Sales teams must master new skills related to various technologies to manage and engage their audience effectively online. Navigating virtual sales meetings amidst distractions, pitching to a team of buyers online, or resolving client issues with unstable internet connections can be daunting. Yet, this presents an opportunity: new relationships can now be developed entirely online, transcending time zones and reducing international sales travel costs. Evaluate how proficient your sales teams are in using social media. Are their online profiles as professional as they should be? Is your company brand consistently represented online by your sales teams and other functions? Online networks have become crucial in creating awareness and relationships with your brand long before the first interaction between a salesperson and a potential buyer. This new mindset and skill set may necessitate investment in your people and software to maximise tools like WhatsApp, Zoom, Teams, FaceTime and Google Meet. As a result, your business's financial health and growth will increasingly depend on these media and the associated sales skills.

Product / Service Demonstration

Mastering the art of product or service demonstrations is a crucial skill for any sales team, presenting a prime opportunity to showcase the benefits to potential buyers. In high-performing companies, these demonstrations are not just routine presentations but are approached as strategic engagements requiring extensive practice and preparation. These companies excel by adopting a continuous improvement approach, always seeking to enhance their sales demonstration capabilities.

To truly excel in product demonstrations, a sales team must:

- Thoroughly rehearse product features and benefits. This ensures a smooth, polished presentation that effectively communicates the value proposition. Rehearsing helps anticipate potential questions and prepare convincing answers, making the demonstration an interactive and engaging experience.

- Develop a compelling elevator pitch. A well-crafted elevator pitch is crucial. It should succinctly convey the unique selling points of the product or service, instantly capturing the attention and interest of potential customers.

- In-depth product or service knowledge. A thorough understanding of the product's capabilities and limitations is vital. This knowledge enables the team to confidently address any questions or concerns during the demonstration, enhancing credibility and trustworthiness.

- Tailor demonstrations to customer needs. Customising the demonstration to align with the customer's specific challenges and pain points illustrates how the product or service can provide solutions and tangible benefits. This approach shifts the demonstration from a generic presentation to a personalised experience for the prospect.

- Learn from each demonstration. Successful teams continuously refine their demonstration techniques. They analyse what resonates with customers and what could be improved, sharing these insights across the team to elevate collective performance.

- If your sales team struggles with delivering effective product or service demonstrations, it can significantly impact their ability to convert prospects into customers and it affects the overall success and growth of the business. Demonstrations that fail to effectively showcase the value of the product or service can leave potential customers unconvinced and even raise doubts about the company's competence.

Opportunity Identification

Identifying and capitalising on the right sales opportunities is a critical task for sales and marketing teams and scoring high in this area signifies that a company has a comprehensive customer, prospect, and buyer profiling process. These companies utilise feedback loops and performance evaluation to refine their approach continuously.

Effective opportunity identification involves:

- Continuous target market and prospect research. This research is fundamental for understanding current and potential customers. It involves analysing pain points, preferences and purchasing behaviour. It enables sales and marketing teams to devise strategies tailored to each target segment.
- Developing customer advocacy and third-party referral systems. Establishing these systems is vital for successful lead generation. By nurturing relationships with satisfied customers and encouraging them to share their positive experiences, companies can organically expand their reach and credibility in the market.

Collaborations with partners, influencers, or industry experts can provide valuable endorsements and further bolster the brand's reputation.

- A systematic approach to lead generation. This approach should be grounded in thorough research, customer advocacy, strategic partnerships and sales training. It's about creating a well-rounded strategy that ensures better and more consistent outcomes.

A below-benchmark performance in this area can indicate a lack of proper understanding of the target market and prospects, potentially leading to wasted efforts on unqualified leads or ineffective sales strategies. It might also signify that the sales team is not adequately profiling customers and buyers, which can result in missed opportunities and a failure to communicate the value proposition of products or services effectively.

Understanding Needs

In the world of sales, the ability to effectively discern a customer's underlying desires and necessities is often what distinguishes a successful sales engagement. The days are gone when the product was the only thing that mattered and customers felt a sense of need to bend their own needs to the almighty product. Now it's entirely about the customer and their specific needs to solve their specific problems that drive the ship. If a company can't offer the flexibility to solve the problem, the customer simply moves on to the next company in line.

High-performing sales professionals excel in the art of discovery and inquiry, guiding customers to articulate their challenges, comprehend the tangible impact of these issues on their operations and identify underlying causes. Central to this process is a commitment to value-based solution development. This approach involves an ongoing process evaluation and refinement cycle, ensuring solutions are precisely tailored to meet the customer's unique requirements. Harnessing customer feedback is invaluable in maintaining alignment with the customer journey and driving enhancements in performance. Sales professionals facing challenges in these skills may find it difficult to pinpoint customers' true needs and obstacles, potentially leading to solutions that fall short of fully addressing customer concerns. Consequently, the company might face lower conversion rates, missed sales opportunities and a decline in market reputation. Weak discovery and questioning abilities could result in an incomplete grasp of the customer's business environment, hindering the sales team's capacity to tailor offerings effectively. Customers perceiving a lack of expertise or understanding of their needs may turn to competitors offering more targeted solutions.

Developing customer-centric solutions requires innovative thinking, meticulous attention to detail and ongoing customer purchasing behaviours and business dynamics monitoring. Selling effectively revolves around aiding customers in reaching their goals. Understanding the challenges, implications and needs of each stakeholder in the purchasing group, along with their individual and collective roles in the decision-making process, is crucial. The aim is not merely to sell but to understand the customer journey thoroughly, thereby creating value, identifying needs, and positioning oneself as a trusted advisor.

For sales teams underperforming in this area, reassessing their sales methodology is crucial. It is essential to ensure that effective questioning techniques to uncover customer needs are well-documented, regularly updated and informed by practical feedback. Encouraging consistent practice and sharing of these techniques, regardless of geographical location, is key to improving these skills.

Proposals and Tenders

Managing proposals and tenders reflects an organisation's proficiency in handling these complex yet crucial components. Best practices in this domain demand well-trained sales and support teams, streamlined processes and efficient systems. The ability to quickly access response data, utilise standardised proposal templates and adapt to varying prospect scenarios using a flexible RFP database are marks of a company adept in this area.

Responding to tenders and large contracts is a sophisticated process that often begins long before the formal RFP stage. Teams that consistently secure significant contracts are known for their proactive engagement with customers or prospects and refined response strategies, supported by a centralised and accessible information hub. RFPs, despite their varying formats, generally seek consistent core information about the company, such as its financial stability, operational capabilities and historical background. An organised and efficient response strategy is pivotal in positioning a company to acquire substantial contracts and elevate its sales performance successfully. Crafting an effective proposal or RFP response and closing a contract require specific expertise. A collaborative team approach, leveraging diverse strengths and specialised knowledge, is often the most successful strategy for intricate tenders. In cases like international businesses, gathering information might necessitate input from various regions or external experts. If your team's performance in this area is not meeting benchmarks, it is advisable to reassess the effectiveness of your information gathering, proposal completion and RFP response processes. While tenders can be lucrative, they demand significant resources and time. Establishing clear criteria for when to engage in tenders is key to optimising resource use.

Standardising response processes can appear daunting, but it begins with understanding the commonalities in information requests. Maintaining a central repository with pre-formulated answers to frequent queries can significantly streamline the response process.

Success in responding to tenders and RFPs requires a team proficient in RFP response, equipped with standardised proposal templates and supported by a versatile RFP database. This setup should allow the flexibility to cater to specific prospect scenarios and specialised subjects, ensuring the organisation's agility and competitiveness in this demanding sales aspect.

Negotiation

Achieving proficiency in negotiation is a hallmark of high-scoring sales teams, indicative of a culture steeped in continuous learning, training and effective coaching. Negotiation, an indispensable skill in the sales arsenal, demands a delicate balance of preparation, strategic planning and keen understanding of customer needs and preferences. It's an intricate dance of give-and-take that seeks to reach a mutually beneficial agreement.

Effective negotiation involves a series of well-orchestrated steps:

- Comprehensive Planning and Preparation. Understanding the customer's requirements, anticipating potential objections and formulating strategies are foundational. It's about entering the negotiation with a clear roadmap yet being adaptable to the dynamic nature of customer interactions.

- Clarifying and Justifying Positions. The ability to articulate your stance convincingly is critical, while also empathetically acknowledging the customer's viewpoint. This dual approach ensures that negotiations are grounded in mutual understanding and respect.

- Active Listening and Assertiveness. Master negotiators balance assertiveness with active listening. They command the conversation when necessary yet remain attuned to the customer's feedback, ensuring a two-way dialogue.

- Bargaining and Problem-Solving. Negotiations often involve trade-offs. Skilful sales representatives navigate this by making well-considered concessions, brainstorming creative solutions and steering discussions towards scenarios where both parties emerge as winners. This collaborative approach not only seals deals but also lays the groundwork for enduring customer relationships, enhancing satisfaction and paving the way for future business and referrals.

Should your team's negotiation skills need bolstering, the focus should shift to strategic actions to refine their approach. This includes understanding the customer's buying process, recognising that price is not always pivotal and exploring value-added options before price concessions. Providing clear pricing and discounting strategies guidelines and fostering an assertive yet composed demeanour, are crucial for steering negotiations to successful conclusions.

Deal Closure

The closure of a deal is often a defining moment, yet it's the culmination of a meticulously executed series of actions. High-performing sales teams understand that the art of closing a deal extends beyond the final handshake or signature. It's an ongoing process that begins much earlier in the sales cycle and continues well after signing the deal.

To drive successful deal closures, a comprehensive approach is essential:

- Building Strong Customer Relationships. Throughout the sales process, it's imperative to establish a deep understanding of the customer's needs, tailor solutions accordingly and maintain a supportive presence even after the deal is closed. This consistent engagement fosters trust and lays a solid foundation for future transactions.

- Addressing Early Stage Challenges. If a sales team struggles with closing deals, the root cause often lies earlier in the sales process. It could be linked to the initial identification of opportunities, a lack of effective questioning techniques, or a failure to demonstrate the product or service's value adequately.

- Structured Approach to Product Trials. Ensuring that product trials are conducted with clear objectives, defined processes and measurable outcomes is vital. Both parties should have a mutual understanding of what constitutes success or failure in a trial and the next steps post-trial.
- Mastering Closing Techniques. Different scenarios call for different closing strategies. Sales representatives should be adept in various techniques, from assumptive closes to time-limited offers and know when to apply each method effectively.

In cases where deal closures are not meeting expectations, it's critical to identify the stages requiring improvement. Providing targeted training, coaching and support in areas such as negotiation, opportunity identification and effective product or service presentation can significantly enhance the team's overall performance, leading to more successful deal closures.

The aim is to develop a sales team that is well-versed in closing techniques and excels in communication, rapport-building, active listening and understanding customer values. This holistic approach ensures that deal closures are not just transactions but the culmination of a well-nurtured relationship and a testament to the team's comprehensive sales acumen.

Pillar 6: Sales Enablement and Technology

Sales enablement is a key component of a high-performing sales organisation. A high performance in this area indicates that a company recognises the importance of equipping its sales team with the necessary tools, resources and training to sell their product or service effectively. This includes combining well-structured support systems, targeted training, valuable content, and powerful analytical tools.

Key strategies for effective sales enablement include:

- Comprehensive Training and Development. Ensuring the sales team is thoroughly trained in the products or services' features, benefits and applications. Training should be ongoing, adapting to new product releases and market shifts.

- Developing Standardised Demonstration Processes and Best Practices. Establishing a consistent, high-quality approach across the sales team enhances the effectiveness of product demonstrations and customer interactions.

- Personalisation of Sales Approaches. Encouraging sales people to customise their demonstrations and sales tactics based on each prospect's unique needs and challenges, thereby highlighting the product's or service's relevance and value.

- Ongoing Coaching and Support. Continuous

support to sales representatives helps them refine their presentation and communication skills, which are essential for successful customer engagements.

- Regularly Reviewing and Updating Sales Materials. Keeping demonstration materials and sales processes up to date ensures that the sales team remains aligned with evolving customer needs and industry trends.

If your company has low performance in sales enablement, it can lead to a range of challenges, from reduced sales performance and slowed business growth to decreased morale among the sales team. Without the proper support and resources, sales representatives may struggle to achieve their targets, potentially leading to higher employee turnover and the associated costs of recruiting and training new staff. Therefore, a comprehensive sales enablement strategy is crucial for empowering your sales team and driving exceptional results.

Sales Enablement

Providing your sales team with the tools and resources to effectively sell your product or service is essential for exceptional sales performance. High-performing organisations understand the importance of combining supportive systems, targeted training, relevant content and analytical tools. Such organisations adopt a systematic approach to enhancing sales productivity, offering personalised training and development plans and utilising data on customer interactions for informed decision-making.

If your company's performance is low in sales enablement, it may result in reduced sales performance and slower business growth. This can lead to decreased morale among sales staff, higher employee turnover and additional costs for hiring and training new staff.

An effective sales enablement strategy should include standardised documentation and customer communication processes. A comprehensive sales playbook outlining best practices for each sales cycle stage supports consistency and success in sales efforts. Standardising these elements is a critical starting point for improving your sales enablement strategy. Review the key stages of customer engagement and streamline processes for efficiency and effectiveness. Implementing LEAN process maps and documenting these processes can help identify areas for simplification. Enhancing your sales enablement approach can create a more consistent and efficient sales team, improving customer satisfaction and stronger business performance.

Integrating technology into sales and customer service teams can be a game-changer, significantly influencing adaptability, knowledge, performance and customer relationships. In top-tier companies, there's a seamless fusion of technological systems spanning customer interfaces, sales engagement, marketing, customer service, delivery, and finance.

These organisations typically adopt sales enablement and customer-centric CRM systems that align with well-thought-out sales policies and processes. This infrastructure provides sales teams with timely information, enhancing sales activities. For instance, real-time inventory access via management information systems aids salespeople, customers and channel partners. Additionally, financial systems divulge crucial sales and profit data, aiding in precise planning and forecasting. A key feature in these high-performing companies is integrating mobile solutions, offering access to critical data anytime, anywhere. This technological empowerment allows sales representatives to connect with global buyers and sell products from almost any location. Sharing information in diverse formats boosts personal effectiveness, decision-making and communication. However, it's essential to recognise that technology is not a panacea for all sales challenges. Even the most advanced systems cannot compensate for these fundamental deficiencies if sales processes, workflows and integration objectives are unclear or suboptimal. It's common for companies to invest heavily in state-of-the-art systems only to find them underutilised or incapable of delivering necessary information at critical junctures. Similarly, outdated or makeshift CRM systems can create additional burdens for sales and customer teams.

If your organisation's performance isn't meeting the upper quartiles, it may signal unoptimised underlying processes or inadequately implemented technology.

In our increasingly digital world, where social networks are the new boardrooms, sales professionals must master digital media as a selling and networking tool. Proficiency in leveraging social networks for cross-selling or upselling, email tracking, web conferencing and advanced computer skills — like customer analytics and database management — is essential for remaining competitive globally.

Before jumping to procure the latest technology, it's wise to reevaluate your organisation's information workflows. Understanding how data moves between your organisation, customers, and sales prospects is critical. Once these foundational aspects are addressed, technology solutions can be implemented to bolster performance and productivity.

Management Information Systems

In the digital age, data is the lifeblood of a company and effective data management is integral to strategic performance. Forward-thinking organisations invest in sophisticated information systems to secure a competitive edge, driven by quality data that informs superior decision-making. The value of accurate, timely, and relevant information cannot be overstated, as it is vital for informed decision-making across all business domains. These systems are crucial, whether it's for financial management, production, internal processes, customer service, or sales and marketing. The effectiveness of management information systems hinges on the quality and timeliness of the data they provide. Consequently, organisations should prioritise optimising their data infrastructure to ensure information is current and accessible to decision-makers.

Advanced information systems enable organisations to make strategic decisions, fostering growth and success. Efficient data management supports decision-making, cultivates innovation, enhances collaboration and empowers a faster response to market demands.

Accessible sales analytics and reporting can profoundly impact performance and customer satisfaction. Conversely, poor performance in this area can detrimentally affect sales outcomes. The quality of information regarding the market, sales activities, customer preferences, inventory and delivery directly influences sales effectiveness. Service quality depends on timely and accurate data about responsiveness, reliability, empathy, competence and overall quality. The disparity between customer expectations and the service delivered can be the difference between developing loyal advocates and a high customer attrition rate.

In a world of information, efficient data management systems become crucial to prevent confusion and disorder. With vast market and customer data available through social media channels, sales and marketing teams must effectively utilise this information. For instance, with LinkedIn's vast user base, sales professionals must know how to identify and connect with target customers. It is vital to use digital platforms and social media channels effectively for networking, prospect engagement, industry updates and competitive analysis. Enhancing digital skills and leveraging available information are key to improving connections with prospects, closing deals and maintaining customer satisfaction. Failing to do so leaves the door open for competitors to gain the upper hand.

CRM Systems

Incorporating best-practice CRM systems is pivotal for any sales-driven organisation, as they support a broad spectrum of sales methodologies and unique company-specific approaches. This comprehensive support enhances the likelihood of adopting sales practices that are apt, relevant and conducive to success.

High-performing companies utilise CRM systems as powerful tools, enabling salespeople to streamline and optimise their activities. These systems offer instant access to essential sales tools, training and collateral at critical junctures. They centralise a repository of documents for each customer or prospect group, facilitating efficient collaboration in document preparation and development. This centralised approach eliminates redundant searches for the latest document versions and enhances team efficiency.

Effective CRM software empowers sales and marketing teams to deepen customer relationships by better understanding their needs while providing management with robust tools to oversee and guide sales efforts. Comprehensive functionality in CRM systems aids in streamlining sales processes, improving customer engagement and ultimately driving superior outcomes. However, a mismatch between adopted sales practices and the CRM solution can hinder performance. For example, a contact management system designed decades ago may not suffice for complex modern sales requirements. The efficacy of a CRM system relies on understanding and designing processes that augment sales productivity, tailored to each stage of the customer journey and incorporating the necessary resources to advance sales.

Modern CRM systems offer user-friendly flexibility and integrated support, enhancing the accuracy of forecasts and correlating sales activities with results. They are especially valuable in orchestrated team selling scenarios, where multiple personnel collaborate on a sale, connecting the right individuals for each opportunity. CRM systems should facilitate sales processes and integrate tailored best practices, ensuring organisations learn from past experiences to refine their sales strategies continuously.

Sales Enablement Systems

Sales enablement technology systems are crucial for empowering sales teams to access playbook content tailored to their target customers at each sales funnel stage. These systems promote continuous improvement and adherence to best practices, offering a platform for content related to feedback, training, support and analysis.

As sales operations grow more intricate, the demand for robust sales enablement systems has escalated. Equipped with appropriate platforms, sales playbooks, and training support, sales and marketing teams can deliver timely and relevant content to prospects. Sales enablement systems yield substantial benefits: fostering collaboration between marketing and sales, promoting continuous learning, enhancing productivity, and facilitating robust customer engagement. These systems are critical for maintaining a competitive edge in the digital market landscape.

Recent trends have shown a surge in the adoption of sales enablement functions, with over sixty percent of companies now investing in dedicated enablement roles or programs. This move towards virtual enablement, accelerated by the COVID-19 pandemic, has expanded these systems beyond sales, encompassing account management, customer engagement, and channel management. Navigating the growing market of sales enablement software vendors can be daunting. It is vital to discern which solutions align with your business objectives, categorised broadly into sales readiness, asset management and engagement. It is essential to have a clear definition of your business's needs before committing to a specific system. Fundamentally, these systems serve as repositories for marketing collateral and sales playbooks, accessible at the appropriate sales cycle stage. They extend beyond content libraries, offering coaching, training and onboarding platforms, thereby expediting new sales staff's productivity.

Internal and External Connectivity

In the global and digital business arena, interconnectivity is vital for success. Leading organisations create robust networks connecting suppliers, partners and customers, and fostering collaboration and transparency. This technological integration enables the customisation of products and services to individual customer needs and nurtures beneficial relationships.

By leveraging real-time supply and demand data, companies enhance flexibility for channel partners while improving their operational efficiency. This approach reduces costs and increases profitability through quicker order capture, precise planning and streamlined logistics. Such interconnected ecosystems enable sharing insights and driving innovation, helping businesses to adapt swiftly to market changes. As a result, companies that embrace technological integration can better anticipate and meet customer needs, boosting satisfaction and sales.

Organisations scoring lower in systems integration face challenges like organisational silos, complex processes and fragmented systems, that leads to reduced profitability and customer satisfaction. The issue often arises from independently developed systems like CRM, supply chain management and sales force automation systems – especially in multinational corporations with localised systems in each region.

Addressing technology challenges in today's interconnected economy is crucial for competitiveness and growth. The pandemic has emphasised the need to re-evaluate business operations. Companies must now focus on reducing costs, improving productivity and aligning with evolving customer expectations. The first steps in this transformation are to assess current systems, identify gaps and seize improvement opportunities.

Sales Dashboards

High-performing teams deploy comprehensive dashboards that are actively used, dynamically updated and routinely reviewed to guarantee the content's quality relevance, and impact. These dashboards provide essential data the sales team can readily access and practically apply.

Top-tier companies distinguish themselves by

accessing real-time performance data linked to individual, departmental, or functional goals. This feature is prevalent across high-growth companies of various sizes. They establish clear objectives and disseminate these goals alongside corresponding OKRs (Objectives and Key Results) or KPIs (Key Performance Indicators) throughout the organisation. These metrics offer critical insights into the company's progress at every level, ensuring the business remains on course.

Incorporating well-structured sales dashboards allows companies to monitor performance, persistently enabling informed, data-driven decisions. This approach aligns individual and organisational goals, fostering improved decision-making and elevating overall performance. As technology evolves, it affords the extraction of detailed data. The real challenge lies in pinpointing the key data that reveals performance drivers, allowing prompt corrective actions. Discovering a revenue target missed halfway through a six-month sales cycle, with no opportunities in the pipeline's latter stages, is too late for effective action. If your business performance is lower in this area, it may indicate a gap in effectively generating and analysing performance data. This gap could stem from not asking the right questions to understand prospecting activities or current customer engagement levels.

Understanding the most effective sales processes for customer acquisition, engagement and retention is pivotal. Tracking the key performance indicators driving optimal performance is essential. Identifying areas of underperformance at the outset of the sales pipeline conversion process is crucial. Understanding the specifics of failing conversion metrics allows for targeted coaching and performance improvement.

Performance dashboards in other domains, like manufacturing and inventory management, are heavily influenced by accurate sales forecasting and optimal customer engagement. It's critical to develop proficient sales dashboards to understand a business's current performance and assess the impact of measures taken to recover or improve outcomes. Limited sales dashboards, or those designed only for specific meetings and reports, often mean that sales teams lack the insights needed to identify their weaknesses, whether as a team or individually. By addressing these deficiencies and implementing robust sales dashboards, organisations can enable their sales teams to make informed, data-driven decisions and foster continuous performance improvement.

Case Study: Sharing Global Best Practices

Global businesses can each have hundreds of thousands of suppliers. Managing those suppliers is very complex: for example, ensuring they have the right quality standards, accreditations, or social and environmental policies in line with global policies and expectations.

A private equity firm had recently acquired this group and believed that, though it was profitable, it was seriously underperforming its market potential. Its sales were growing in some countries by as much as twenty-five percent per annum, but this was inconsistent across different countries. The company had a major account field sales team in each country and several hundred internal sales people managing sales to the suppliers. The investors were right about its market potential because, as it turned out, in the end, we increased sales by forty-eight percent within two years and delivered nineteen percent annual net profits. The challenge was figuring out how, why and where they were underperforming, creating an effective growth plan for each country and then motivating the business to deliver extraordinary results. It took a team of five people, including me, almost four months to audit their sales and marketing teams across six continents and twenty-three countries. This was all about designing and delivering a transformative journey in sales practices and strategies in a global business.

Our journey began with an ambitious undertaking: introducing a Sales Best Practices (SBP) programme across six diverse business regions, twenty-three countries, one hundred and sixty-eight field sales people and approximately three hundred internal telephone sales professionals. English was a common language at a managerial level, but this was not the case amongst each local country team. This programme marked a significant shift in their approach, revamping their sales practices and laying the groundwork for future growth. It was a holistic initiative that sought to align its sales strategies with core business drivers, including customer acquisition, customer engagement, supply chain campaigns and product upselling. The organisation operated as a federation of businesses, which tended to create a lack of synergy and practical coordination. However, the SBP programme was poised to bridge these gaps, standardising practices and establishing a unified approach across diverse business regions while maintaining flexibility to reflect local needs. It was a transformational initiative to unite the organisation's strengths and provide a blueprint for future success.

We began by assessing the sales performance numbers as best we could, although historical sales and product performance data across the regions were sparse. Each region had its own unique set of sales data, none of which was comprehensive or comparable. Data on sales performance was scarce, particularly regarding sales by individual salespeople and customer sales across different regions. This lack of detailed information posed a significant challenge. We examined individual profiles, backgrounds, specialisations and experiences, analysing processes from target identification to market analysis and pre-sales efforts. Our goal was to unravel the strengths and weaknesses of their sales process, the dynamics within their sales teams and how they engaged with customers and critical stakeholders. The first phase of our engagement involved change management workshops designed around their core business drivers. including customer acquisition and customer engagement, supply chain campaigns and product upsell. These elements were identified as critical components of the strategy to drive future growth. They formed the cornerstone of our efforts to transform the organisation's sales practices, paving the way for harmonisation, upskilling and integrating best practices identified during the earlier research phase that year. Not surprisingly, we found many more examples of excellence as we went from region to region.

With the first workshops focussing on core sales processes, activity-based measurement and sales planning, we needed to build on that in the next stage, addressing Account Management skils and responsibilities and a detailed review of each country's customer and prospect portfolio. For selling skills development, we included multiple video role-play sessions where the sales people got to play buyer and seller in a bid to up-sell several cf their key products and services as was appropriate to each region. Strangely, sales people who are normally gregarious and engaging people suddenly become camera shy when practising with their colleagues. However, as with most teams I have worked with, they soon realise that everyone feels the same and then get fully engaged. This practical training and coaching type is always enjoyable and usually extremely successful. The key is to select real customer or prospect situations and challenges already in the sales pipeline and then help them succeed – capturing attention more than anything.

Sales, at its core, is about people. We needed to

understand the human element within their sales teams. Who were the key players? What roles did they play? How well-structured were these teams? We explored the dynamics of their sales teams – both field-based and internal. How much time did they invest in particular customers or customer groups? Who else should be involved in the process? It was about creating a cohesive, well-oiled machine. Identifying the skills required at different stages of the sales process was paramount. Equally important was understanding how these skills were nurtured within their teams. Did they have a playbook? Was there any standard set of pitch documents? We delved into their skills development and training initiatives. It was about understanding how they transformed raw talent into sales champions. Training, knowledge sharing and technology all involved this process.

As we embarked on this transformative journey, travelling from one region to another, what became evident was nothing short of remarkable: Each region offered unique insights and the teams' dedication to excellence was inspiring. It was more than a simple alignment of processes; it was a profound shift in mindset, fostering a shared commitment to high-performance sales practices. In the subsequent stages of our engagement, we delved deeper into the nuances of Account Management skills and responsibilities. Here, the goal was to ensure that the teams understood their roles and had a detailed understanding of their respective customer and prospect portfolios.

Furthermore, we looked into the criteria or framework they utilised to assess the attractiveness of a particular customer or customer group. Understanding their approach was vital as their sales involved complex procedures – not just selling to individual companies but bringing multiple large organisations together. We needed to understand what made their strategies successful, including how they gathered information about the market, its size, key contacts, the extent of their supply chains and any forthcoming contracts in the market they could potentially capitalise on. Our examination extended to how they conducted their meetings and discussions, their preparation for these interactions with customer groups and understanding whether their approach involved dealing with these organisations individually or was more effective when collectively engaging a group of these companies. We also looked at the duration from securing these meetings to the point where they managed to get commitments, including the length of the process and the number of meetings required to secure a group agreement.

The process was quite intensive. They developed multiple contacts within these large organisations, necessitating significant pre-sales effort. However, the payoff was substantial – once a deal was signed, it led to deep commitment within these organisations. One of their challenges was balancing achieving a quicker sale with securing greater depth and income in the later stages of account management. Therefore, we examined which industry sectors were particularly successful and which weren't, the reasons for failure and the lessons learned from these experiences. We also looked into the best practices adopted, the technology for gathering and analysing data and how deeply they needed to penetrate these organisations to secure commitment. In selling to major organisations, identifying the key stakeholders was crucial, and often, there could be many — on average, anywhere from fifteen to thirty different stakeholders in the buying process. One of the most significant insights was whether the sales team conducted thorough, in-depth research and understood the target customer base. It turned out that this company was quite adept at this, at least in some parts of the world.

For the best practice programme to be effective, we needed to understand how they convinced major corporate buyers to collaborate and then set up a process with standard engagement letters and methods. This part involved understanding both the people aspect and the organisational structure. Who in the organisation initiated engagements? Who was part of the company team, considering that the sales were not individual but required a team effort? We examined how well these teams were structured in their respective roles, the time devoted by team members to particular customers or groups and who else should be involved in the process. Importantly, we researched the skills needed at different sales process stages — from identification through discovery, demos, proposals, etc. We looked into how they identified these skills in their people, the training provided and the frequency of updating knowledge and skills among the sales teams.

Moving into the area of technology and tools enabling them to perform their roles efficiently, we found they had a very complex CRM system. However, this system was not primarily designed for ease of use by the salespeople but for the operational aspects of the business and its financial management. One of the challenges was extracting information about how the sales people carried out their jobs in terms of methodologies. It was noted that different parts of the world had different approaches to selling in a complex environment. Some used methodologies like Miller Heiman, while others employed various other forms of solution selling. Understanding the required support material, the research needed, and who would do this was equally important. Was there a playbook or any standard set of pitch documents? This comprehensive analysis provided a deep insight into the sales teams' current state and laid the groundwork for targeted improvements and strategies for future success.

A vital characteristic of this business was its requirement to strengthen customer engagement capabilities rather than merely seeking new customers. They were uniquely positioned with abundant opportunities, making the critical question not about finding opportunities but selecting the right ones to pursue. This scenario was atypical compared to many companies.

Some of the hurdles we overcame included:

- A large CRM system was designed to deliver their operational services and not as a sales performance measurement tool.
- It was hard to get measurable data about past performance at a sales team, salesperson, country, customer, or product level. The data was financially and operationally structured rather than related to sales performance or activity.
- The divisions operated like a federation of independent businesses with little cohesion or cross-learning.
- One of the country sales teams who were performing well had great resistance to the idea of anyone coming in from the outside telling them they needed to improve.
- The majority of the major projects had been initiated by the sales director and the managing director, but not so much by the sales teams.
- The positives we took away from the experience:
- The business had many very capable and motivated people.
- The acquisition meant more investment and no reduction in the workforce.
- All regions except one were enthusiastic about the "Best practice programme" we were running.
- The audit team included me and four highly

capable people.

- There was a considerable opportunity for growth.
- The company was developing several new "upsell" product streams.

Sales Pipeline Visibility

One of the many notable moments as we worked our way across the regions, included when we went to work with the teams in southern Europe about halfway through their financial year. They were doing OK as a business and were keen to engage in the best practice programme.

During one of our sessions, we examined the depth and strength of their sales pipeline. This was a business that historically had a sixteenth month sales cycle, so it was critical to understand exactly what stage each opportunity was at, the determining factors leading to a likely close or not and, importantly, how long this would take. Although they had a healthy number of good-quality prospects, it soon became clear that they would miss their annual target significantly on their present trajectory. There were simply not enough opportunities at the right stage in the sales cycle to close within the following six months and hit their business targets. We still had time to resolve this, but it meant swift and decisive action to focus on all opportunities that stood any chance of being closed before the year-end and sifting out the ones that could not.

We increased the volume and focus of activity for the internal and field-based sales team, using a small multi-function team approach to work on the more complex deals that had multiple stakeholders in the client buying group. Each week for about two months we would have check-in sessions to learn what progress they had made and overcome any challenges. Thankfully, about two months later, they were back on track and ended the year almost thirty percent ahead of plan. The lesson learned was to ensure you have total visibility and understanding of sales pipeline dynamics.

There were similar stories of remarkable people in the Nordics, Germany and other countries. In Germany, they were particularly good at managing complex accounts and soon developed the skills to upsell other products and services. At the other end of the world were the teams in Latin America. This was an important part of the change programme and we had carefully planned almost two weeks of coaching and development for the local management and their respective teams. Two of us had flown fifteen hours from London to Santiago and stayed in the Hotel "Panamericano" in the city centre. No sooner had we arrived than we were whisked off to meet the teams from Argentina and Brazil: about forty people in one room with a small cabin in one corner housing two interpreters. We introduced ourselves and the sales best practice programme with each wearing headsets. It was a resounding success. They were extremely keen to learn, despite their world-class skills and process around client acquisition, skills and practices that we later transferred to the rest of the group countries and teams. We brought them new and better account management practices, some from Germany and others from within our programme. The net result was a dramatic increase in customer growth and upselling in the next twelve months.

Having come that far around the world, unusually, we did manage to squeeze in one day walking up the San Cristóbal Hill to see the famous statue of the Virgin Mary, towering almost one thousand feet over the slightly misty Santiago city skyline. As any of you fellow business globe-trotters will know, getting any time actually to see the places we travel to is a rarity, as usually it simply means getting up at some unearthly hour to catch an early flight to a hotel somewhere else in the world. Then I went into business meetings before eventually returning on a flight back home, having messed up my body clock in different time zones.

The Takeaways

There are so many things to learn from this experience that are just as relevant in the global clients we have worked with ever since.

Auditing as a Foundation for Improvement:

- The extensive audit of the global supply chain business services company across six continents and twenty-three countries highlights the importance of thorough evaluation as a foundation for improving sales and marketing strategies.

Adapting to Complex Global Markets:

- Operating in global markets requires great adaptability and visibility with stringent compliance measures, allowing for localisation. So often, the challenge for multinational companies is the left hand not knowing what the right hand is doing, creating sub-optimisation, waste and restricting growth potential.

Leveraging Scale and Efficiency:

- This company's strategy to group several large organisations and manage common suppliers for efficiency and scale is a significant lesson in maximising resources and creating cost-effective solutions.

Identifying Underperformance and Potential:

- Recognizing that a company, despite being profitable, is underperforming its market potential underlines the necessity of assessing current success and identifying latent potential.

Challenges in Sales Process and Performance Measurement:

- The hurdles like a CRM system not being tailored for sales performance measurement and the lack of cohesive operation across divisions underscore the importance of having the right tools and organisational synergy for effective management.

Leveraging Internal Resources and New Investments:

- Utilising capable and motivated personnel, alongside new investments without workforce reduction, demonstrates the importance of internal resource optimisation and strategic investment in growth.

Sharing Best Practices:

- The rollout of the Best Practices programme across diverse regions highlights the significance of standardising sales practices and aligning them with business drivers like customer acquisition and engagement.

Overcoming Language and Cultural Barriers:

- Addressing the challenges of implementing a unified sales programme in a multilingual, multicultural environment underlines the importance of cultural sensitivity, localised best practices and effective communication in global business operations.

Transformative Training and Skill Development:

- The focus on real client and prospect role-playing and practical training for sales teams illustrates the effectiveness of experiential learning and real-world application in developing sales skills.

Understanding and Structuring Sales Teams:

- Analysing the structure of sales teams and their

customer engagement emphasises the need for well-organised and cohesive team dynamics in sales.

Strategic Customer Engagement and Selection:

- A focused approach to strengthening customer engagement and strategically selecting opportunities points to the importance of quality over quantity in client targeting and relationship building.

Sales Pipeline Management:

- The emphasis on visibility and understanding of the sales pipeline, as seen in the case of the teams in southern Europe, showcases the criticality of proactive pipeline management in meeting sales targets.

Local Adaptation and Global Integration:

- The experiences in Latin America and other regions highlight the need for local adaptation of sales practices while ensuring they align with the global strategy.

Holistic Improvement and Continuous Learning:

- The overall outcome of shortened sales cycles, improved processes and a significant increase in sales underscores the benefits of a holistic and continuous learning approach in sales practices.

This experience in the transformative world of Global Best Practices demonstrates the challenges of scaling and innovating in a complex global market.

Managing a global sales operation and the strategies to overcome various challenges are complex. The emphasis on practical solutions, adaptability, and the importance of local nuances and global strategies provides valuable insights for businesses in multinational markets.

Pillar 7: Sales Channels

Sales channels represent businesses' diverse pathways to reach and sell to their customers, encompassing digital and traditional platforms. These channels might include direct sales, retail, online platforms, wholesale, etc. The core aim of employing sales channels is establishing a link between the business and its customers, facilitating access to products or services while generating revenue. Managing these channels effectively involves more than choosing the right avenues; it encompasses the strategic operation and continual assessment of these channels to maximise their performance. It also involves a lot of flexibility, as the way people want to be communicated with is starting to change much more than it used to. The Big Three — TV, radio and print advertisements — dominated the landscape for decades before the advent of the Internet. Now, we have a continually growing number of ways of communication — texting and messaging and any number of social media sites that rise and fall in popularity like the tides.

Proper channel management involves strategic planning, setting and monitoring performance metrics and nurturing relationships with channel partners. When managed skilfully, sales channels can increase sales, expand market reach and enhance profitability. Selecting and managing the right channel partners is a critical task. The advantages and challenges of different sales channels vary depending on the nature of the business and the industry context. Optimal channel management involves carefully choosing suitable channels, evaluating and refining them over time and cultivating strong partnerships to ensure the best outcomes for the business.

<u>Whether large or small, channel partners are an extension of your sales force and brand ambassadors to your end customers</u>. They expect quality products, efficient service and delivery, profitable margins, marketing support and training. Similarly, businesses should anticipate clear commercial agreements, sales plans, forecasts and dedicated sales efforts from their partners. This symbiotic relationship should be mutually beneficial, with shared responsibilities and rewards.

Key elements driving successful sales channel performance include:

- Strategic Channel Planning. Establishing a clear vision and strategy for channel development tailored to the unique needs of the business and market.

- Selecting Appropriate Partners. Choosing the right types and numbers of partners to complement the business model and market demands.

- Optimisation of Activities and Processes. Continuously refining channel activities and processes to ensure efficiency and effectiveness.

- Building Strong Relationships. Developing and maintaining robust relationships with channel partners, fostering trust and collaboration.

- Support Programs for Channel Sales and Marketing. Implementing programs to support partners in sales and marketing efforts, enhancing their ability to represent and sell the products effectively.

- Product and Service Alignment. Tailoring products and services to suit the characteristics of different partner types or geographical locations.

- Engaging Partners Effectively. Ensuring optimum partner engagement through outstanding service delivery and comprehensive support.

By focusing on these drivers, sales teams can effectively manage their distribution channels, leading to increased growth and profitability.

Channel Planning and Strategy

Effective channel planning and strategy in sales distribution channels is a cornerstone of high-performing sales teams. It involves collaborative efforts where sales teams, marketing departments and channel partners work harmoniously, underpinned by well-defined plans that all involved understand and embrace. These plans typically feature multi-level partner strategies, which include regular performance reviews at each level, strategies for geographic expansion and product growth programs tailored to specific market needs.

Strategic sales channel management plans must clearly define the business and channel goals, fostering a sense of shared purpose and direction. The establishment of a mutual achievement plan with channel partners is critical. The plan should outline expectations, responsibilities, timelines and envisioned outcomes. It's imperative that these elements are not only specific and measurable but also realistically attainable, fostering an environment of collaboration and shared accountability. A comprehensive, well-thought-out channel plan enhances communication, aligns goals and drives superior results. This collaborative approach ensures that all parties involved are united in their efforts, working synergistically towards shared success and fostering robust, enduring partnerships that benefit all stakeholders.

Addressing underperformance in channel management involves several key steps. Start with thoroughly analysing your target market to develop efficient channel management strategies. Understand the specific characteristics of your target customers, including their demographics, behaviours, preferences, and buying patterns. Evaluate your existing sales channels by scrutinising their performance, identifying successes and pinpointing improvement areas. Consider adopting new sales channels that align with your business objectives and resonate with your target market. This process involves careful consideration of qualification criteria and the steps necessary to effectively set up, onboard and enable new channel partners for success. Reflect on the necessity of diverse channels to optimise market reach and fulfil your business objectives. Look for opportunities to enhance each sales channel and create seamless customer experiences across all touchpoints. Provide comprehensive training and support for your sales channels, equipping their teams with product knowledge, sales skills and customer service expertise. Ensure your sales team knows each customer segment's unique requirements and the most effective engagement strategies.

Mutual goals, targets and outcomes should be established with your channel partners – utilise data and analytics to make informed decisions about sales channel performance. Identify areas where you can assist them in improving and maximising revenue potential.

I can understand if this all seems a bit dry to you. Many businesses suffer in the planning stage because they are impatient to get to "the good stuff" where they are actually putting boots on the ground and actively engaging the potential customers. But a lack of planning of how that will go is a dangerous proposition because you're assuming that your customers are just idly waiting by the telephone, the front door, or the email login screen waiting for you to grace them with your presence. Think about your typical workday and how much time you have to talk to someone about a product you know only too well they are trying to sell you on. If you haven't done the prep work before you reach out, you'll be lucky to get one foot in the door or one character into their inbox.

In short, if your sales team just shoots from the hip and doesn't plan things out, it's entirely likely that your first best shot turns out to be your only shot and a wasted shot at that! Planning won't win the job for you, but it will give you the best chance to know the customer and plan out your best strategy to succeed.

Case Study: Sales Channels

It's a little bit frightening when you connect with companies that need sales help that seem to have very few salespeople actually working there. It makes you wonder to yourself how they got this far without folding. I've been a part of three or four companies that desperately needed help in channel sales. The first one is a managed IT services business.

The entrepreneurial Founder and Chair of the group was a Steve Jobs type. He always seemed to know what the market was looking for next and found the right product for it just when that market was going to take off. It was a wonder to behold. He always seemed to have the knack of finding the right product at the right time in a market that would grow, and this was one of them. The main company had about a thousand resellers, many of whom were not sufficiently geared up to sell a complex, high-end managed service to a new customer base, targeting Finance and IT Directors. There was a high-touch channel sales team of twelve people and a strong manager who was not from a sales background. Most of this team had not been sufficiently trained and the company had lost faith in them. They were a good team but with mixed skills and not much in the way of sales structure or measurement, but with a really strong manager. The main group business was a well-run, broad-line distribution company hitting about $500 million in annual revenues, with very capable people, great customer service and excellent technologies. That's a vexing situation because it wasn't like you had a ton of bad staffers who couldn't handle the work; instead, a lot of great professionals were being asked to do some fish-out-of-water stuff.

The challenge with this $11 million subset of the main company was that, unlike broad line distribution, the sales process was a more complex business-to-business subscription proposition. This involved several key stakeholders in the customer buying group, including two key players: the Chief Financial Officer (CFO) and the Chief Technical Officer (CTO). The CTO is critical to accepting the technology and the CFO is the main Budget holder. It's like basically every movie you've ever seen where two guys have to turn their key to launch the nuclear weapons from the submarine. You can sweet-talk one of them all day long, but if the other guy isn't feeling your sales pitch (or your pitch to wipe out your enemies with an atom bomb), nothing is going to happen.

I had been invited in originally to train the sales team and manager for a few weeks because sales had stagnated and the main group's Board had lost patience. This was a very high-margin and profitable business in a high-growth market, and it wasn't surprising that the board was pointing fingers at the sales staff and looking for a quick fix. But as a managed services business, it required different sales skills in the channel sales team and their resellers. My initial involvement was framed as a short-term engagement – a few weeks dedicated to training the sales team and their manager. However, there was no sales pipeline visibility or measurement and a noticeable lack of channel management and selling skills. In other words, they wanted me to teach these guys how to play water polo and qualify for the Olympics, only to find out that most of them had never seen the sport, nobody knew the rules and we didn't have any water in the pool. Their sales processes were poor in prospecting, discovery and stakeholder engagement. Fixing most of the issues in the sales team turned out to be easier than expected, thanks to some practical coaching and the solid support of their sales manager. But not everything always went as smoothly as we planned.

To improve their prospecting for example, we asked each team member to bring a list of prospects to a training session. After an hour of some theoretical training, the real challenge began. We gathered around a conference phone and each person took turns making calls to their prospects. You can imagine what they thought of making calls in front of colleagues. I liken it to being a teenager and watching an R-rated film full of nudity and profanity with your parents. Yet, it wasn't long before everyone saw the benefit – learning from each other's experiences. However, one team member was conspicuously absent on one of these afternoon sessions. He didn't have bad gas, nor was he a chain smoker. Instead, we found him – hundred percent real – hiding under the boardroom table rather than facing the phone call. A few years later, I heard he had built a successful marketing business where, fortunately for him, he could leave the prospecting calls to others.

Apart from enhancing sales skills, processes and performance management, we made two key changes that transformed performance outcomes and sales results: The first was recognising that there were distinct market sector characteristics around data management, so we divided the channel sales team into market sector-based specialities and core sectors. We had a team focused on the legal sector, another on local and central government, another on manufacturing and so on. We ended up with four to five different teams. The core data solution remained the same, but the marketing and messaging were realigned to each target customer group. They had a really good marketing team who understood branding but, more importantly, knew about channel marketing and lead generation, what we would now call account-based marketing. This also meant that we could train the individual salespeople to become experts in their respective sectors, often leading industry seminars and conferences.

But here's the real key to the turnaround.

This business was all about channel sales. The group's founder used to say that once in the channel, stay in the channel and never mess around trying to compete with them and your direct sales. The challenge was that they were trying to sell complex managed services through the group's broad-line retailers, which were about high volume and low margins. It was a different skill and mindset from selling in-depth B2B subscriptions. They had about one thousand resellers in the group, but trying to sell complex subscription services through broad-line channel salespeople would not be that effective – hence the stagnation in sales. So we looked at who amongst these resellers was selling well and examined what they were doing and what kind of people and characteristics were making them successful. We profiled them and soon realised we needed a different channel partner. We needed channel partners who were young in their business, were keen, had a different approach to sales, were more flexible and had more understanding of how to sell complex solutions. Out of the original high-volume resellers, we found maybe ten to fifteen who fit the profile. They were smaller, more focused and all entrepreneurial businesses. With this core group, we recruited new partners to end up with thirty resellers aligned to the same key target sectors as our salespeople.

We built the most incredible training programmes and playbooks, coaching the resellers to find and sell to customers. Of course, we put a lot of effort into the tech training, marketing tools and support. We built partner portals for them. We even coached some of them on how to run their businesses and manage their finances, bringing in experts from within the group to help us do that – generally doing everything possible to help them grow.

One critical aspect of this business was the need for any sale to involve consultations with finance and IT personnel. This was pivotal due to the dual nature of the product: it was a technical solution with significant financial implications. Consequently, a closer inspection was often required when sales representatives claimed they were on track to meet their monthly targets or forecasts. During pipeline reviews, we frequently discovered that deals projected to close within two to three weeks were less promising than anticipated. In many cases, sales teams had engaged with IT staff but neglected to consult with the customer finance team. This oversight significantly diminished the likelihood of successfully closing these deals. It underscored the importance of a comprehensive approach to our sales strategy, ensuring all crucial stakeholders were involved in the conversation.

Within a relatively short time of about six to twelve months, we had created about thirty highly proactive and capable channel partners who were part of our team. We had our own specialist channel sales team and partners. They were much better trained, more capable, more of a unified group of people and all specialists in their sectors. This was transformational. The relationship between the core channel sales people and the channel partners was mutual support. Our marketing team would generate leads or the channel partners would find their opportunities. Then, they would bring in one of our expert channel sales teams to work with them on a deal. Some of these deals were significant, running into hundreds of thousands of dollars over a three-year contract period.

That was the key. This was a recurring income business. We made around sixty-five percent gross margin on a three-year deal and delivered maybe eighteen to twenty percent net profit. So, it was a hugely profitable business.

We achieved rapid growth quickly, with the business's annual revenues skyrocketing from £11 million to £25 million in less than two years. Additionally, we secured forward order contracts worth almost £65 million.

Besides good leadership in the core business, the key to our success was the strategic selection of the right partners, coupled with comprehensive training for their management and sales teams. Our focus extended beyond sales training; we also provided extensive marketing, financial, and business management education, tailoring it to enhance our partners' capabilities. This approach resulted in a network of partners who were not only aligned with our goals but were also highly motivated and eager for success. Our journey wasn't without its share of amusing incidents, but overall, the business excelled in every aspect. We offered excellent customer service, maintained a strong product portfolio, and leveraged effective channel marketing in a growing market. A crucial aspect of our strategy was a deep understanding of our sales teams and channel partners' strengths and weaknesses. By elevating their knowledge and skills and meticulously tracking and measuring performance, we were able to collaborate with our partners, driving their success closely. This experience served as a prime example of effectively building and managing a channel network. So often, I meet companies who do not appreciate this and assume that signing up a channel partner means the business will automatically grow. There needs to be a mutual benefit that will add value to the core channel partner offering, not just another badge-collecting exercise for it to work. It takes effort, understanding, and focus together with the channel partner, and then it can be transformative.

Everyone worked hard in this business, but it was also a place with a lot of excitement and funny moments. Even my first day at their headquarters was to set the scene for my next eight years or so working with them.

Channel Mix and Profile

In business-to-business sales channels, strategic focus and clearly defined objectives are paramount. These channels excel when partners are chosen for compatibility, shared values and complementary market presence. This synergy lays the groundwork for a mutually beneficial relationship that bolsters performance across the board.

Communication within these channels is characterised by openness and transparency. Regular meetings and performance reviews are standard practice, ensuring that all parties remain aligned and can promptly address any issues that arise. Ongoing development is also a key focus, with comprehensive training and support provided to the sales team and channel partners. This equips them with the necessary skills and knowledge to effectively sell and support their products or services. Efficient processes are established for lead management, sales operations and customer support. These streamlined processes shorten the sales cycle and greatly enhance customer satisfaction. A customer-centric mindset is adopted, emphasising active listening, personalised experiences and a commitment to exceeding customer expectations at every turn.

Data-driven decision-making is crucial for optimising sales performance and overall channel effectiveness. This approach enables channels to pinpoint areas for improvement and fine-tune their strategies as needed. Adaptability is also a critical attribute, with successful channels being quick to respond to market changes, evolving customer needs and emerging trends, ensuring they remain competitive and poised for growth. Collaboration lies at the heart of high-performing sales channels, fostering a culture that values teamwork and recognises its significant impact on achieving superior results. A long-term vision of nurturing trusting relationships with customers and channel partners underpins ongoing growth and profitability. Conversely, in low-scoring B2B sales channels, the lack of strategic vision and undefined goals leads to disorganisation and inefficiencies among team members and channel partners. Partnerships in these channels are often formed without due diligence or consideration of compatibility, resulting in minimal added value and poor overall performance.

Communication within these channels and with partners tends to be sporadic and unclear, leading to misunderstandings and delayed issue resolution. Inadequate training and support for sales teams and channel partners leave them ill-prepared to effectively sell and support the products or services. Lead management, sales operations and customer support processes are often inefficient or outdated, creating cumbersome sales cycles and reducing customer satisfaction. These channels typically focus on short-term transactions rather than understanding and addressing individual customer needs. Decision-making in underperforming channels is often based on intuition rather than data-driven insights, making it challenging to identify areas for improvement or adjust strategies effectively. As a result, these channels struggle to adapt to market changes, shifting customer needs and emerging trends, leaving them vulnerable to competitive pressures.

Collaboration is frequently weak or non-existent, creating a culture that values individual accomplishments over collective success. This environment prioritises short-term gains over cultivating long-term relationships with customers and channel partners, eroding trust and loyalty and ultimately undermining growth and profitability.

To overcome these challenges, underperforming B2B sales channels must focus on strategic vision, clear goals, effective communication and strong partnerships to achieve mutual growth and success.

Channel Management

A high channel management and efficiency performance indicate a team that expertly optimises sales channel efficiency through streamlined processes. Your team likely enhances performance by implementing quantitative management strategies and monitoring outcomes for quality and success. This proficiency entails aligning responsibilities, goals, KPIs and business objectives with your company's mutual sales targets and desired sales outcomes, guaranteeing consistent efficiency throughout the customer's buying journey, from the initial engagement to measurable results.

Sales channel management is a comprehensive process that includes identifying, selecting, establishing and administering various channels for marketing and selling products or services. This crucial aspect of business strategy requires an in-depth analysis of the target market and competitive landscape to determine the most effective sales channels, both online and offline. Developing well-defined strategies, establishing clear performance metrics and consistently tracking and monitoring sales channel performance are vital components of effective sales channel management. Additionally, it involves nurturing strong relationships with sales channel partners, maximising operational efficiency and proactively addressing and resolving conflicts. When businesses struggle with poor sales channel management, it often stems from a lack of clear strategy, leading to misaligned objectives within the organisation and its channel partners. This can result in an inability to identify the most suitable sales channels, leading to missed opportunities and inefficient resource allocation. Furthermore, weak relationships with channel partners, often due to inadequate communication and collaboration, can foster mistrust and underperformance.

Businesses with suboptimal sales channel management typically fall short in providing sufficient support and training for their internal sales teams and channel partners. The absence of robust and tracked key performance indicators (KPIs) for sales channels hampers the ability to measure success and pinpoint areas for improvement. Resistance to adapting to changing market conditions, customer preferences, or new technologies can place the company at a competitive disadvantage. Inefficient conflict resolution with channel partners can strain relationships and impact performance negatively. This disjointed approach can lead to fragmented customer experiences across different sales channels, damaging the company's reputation and customer satisfaction. Ultimately, businesses with ineffective sales channel management often fail to capitalise on data and analytics for informed decision-making, resulting in missed opportunities for optimisation and growth. Redundant, complex, or non-standardised processes can lead to operational inefficiencies and increased costs, further impeding the company's success in managing its sales channels.

Channel Relationships

A robustly defined, meticulously documented and communicated partner engagement process, embraced by all stakeholders, including partners and channel sales teams, can significantly enhance revenue over time. When everyone within your organisation and the partner community aligns their efforts, you can expect a decrease in conflict and an improvement in customer service as all parties collaborate toward a shared objective. Highly successful companies maintain a well-organised partner ecosystem with clear guidelines and expectations. Without such a structure, partners may lack focus or even work at cross purposes, leading to decreased revenues. Cultivating open communication among all parties involved is essential, allowing the sharing of successes, challenges, and insights on areas that require improvement.

When a team performs poorly and exhibts poor sales channel relationships, they often grapple with issues like ineffective communication and inadequate support. Misunderstandings, confusion, misaligned goals due to communication breakdowns, insufficient training, resources and marketing support can impede channel partners from effectively selling products or services. Unclear expectations and guidelines may lead to inconsistent performance across partners and foster conflicts. Trust building can be challenging under these circumstances, leading to both sides' lack of commitment and cooperation. Moreover, inefficient conflict resolution mechanisms can prolong issues and damage partnerships.

Frequent partner turnover indicates poor sales channel relationships, as dissatisfaction or lack of support drives partners away. Businesses may also face difficulty maintaining partner engagement, leading to reduced collaboration and underperformance. Inconsistent performance due to a lack of well-defined processes and performance metrics can make it difficult for the business to measure and improve its performance. Inadequate incentive structures may fail to effectively motivate channel partners, resulting in suboptimal performance and low satisfaction levels. Poor sales channel relationships can ultimately limit a business's market reach and hinder growth and profitability.

Channel Marketing

Channel marketing, a crucial aspect of business strategy, demands a focused approach that addresses customer preferences and partner objectives. Utilising a broad spectrum of media channels, including traditional and digital platforms, is vital for enhancing brand presence and generating leads. This strategy involves engaging target customer groups with valuable content, setting the stage for increased sales opportunities and brand recognition.

High-performing companies often implement joint marketing programs with channel partners, integrating Market Development Funds (MDF) or Cooperative funding and clearly defined Key Performance Indicators (KPIs) for tracking progress. This approach ensures a unified effort in sales and marketing, fostering strong partnerships between the parent company and its distribution channels.

For channel marketing success, maintaining comprehensive end-to-end processes is key. These include initial customer engagement, winning new business, customer onboarding, upselling, customer retention and encouraging advocacy. The parent company and its channel partners share responsibility for these processes, ensuring integration and continuous optimisation for an effective channel sales and marketing strategy.

In poor channel marketing alignment, the issues often stem from a lack of a cohesive strategy, leading to disorganised marketing efforts and a diluted brand image. This disorganisation can confuse customers, especially when interfacing with third-party channels. Additionally, inadequate support for channel partners may result in underperformance due to ineffective communication and collaboration. A common oversight in suboptimal channel marketing is failing to fully exploit the potential of various media channels, including powerful tools like social media platforms. This underutilisation can limit engagement and brand visibility. Furthermore, neglecting the importance of end-to-end processes can disrupt the customer experience and impede potential growth.

Products and Services

Achieving a high alignment performance in channel products and services typically signifies a strategic focus on developing offerings that meet channel partners' needs. Key to this success is empowering partners with the necessary tools and resources, a feat achieved through comprehensive training and development programs. These initiatives should include workshops, e-learning modules, and practical demonstrations, equipping partners with the knowledge to market and sell your products and services effectively. Top-performing channel businesses develop tailored content strategies, providing channel partners with valuable resources such as case studies, whitepapers and sales collateral. These materials help them effectively communicate the benefits of your products and services and address the unique challenges of their target audience.

Sharing performance analytics and tools with channel partners allows them to monitor and assess their sales activities. These insights enable them to identify areas of strength and improvement, guiding them to refine their sales strategies. Actively involving channel partners in the innovation and development of products and services can yield invaluable feedback from the field, aiding in fine-tuning your offerings to meet market demands. Establishing systematic new product launch plans, including thorough training for channel partners, prepares them to confidently promote and sell your latest products. Conversely, poor management of channel products and services can present numerous challenges. Companies may provide insufficient training and development for channel partners, leading to ineffective representation of products or services. Limited resources and support can hinder channel partners' ability to communicate product benefits effectively. Miscommunication and poor collaboration between the company and its partners can lead to inconsistent performance and strained relationships. Companies often lack the necessary mechanisms to monitor and evaluate partner performance in such scenarios. This gap can lead to missed sales opportunities and inefficient use of resources. Excluding channel partners from the innovation process may result in products not aligning with market needs, affecting customer satisfaction and loyalty. Addressing these issues is vital for maintaining high-quality, competitive products and services, ensuring customer satisfaction and fostering a thriving partnership network.

Operations and Processes

The essence of successful channel and direct sales lies in a customer-centric approach, which hinges on an unwavering commitment to service excellence across all channels. High-performing companies establish and rigorously apply Key Performance Indicators (KPIs) and benchmarks throughout their channel network. This structured approach, often encapsulated in a comprehensive channel sales playbook, ensures that all stakeholders are aligned and adhere to standardised procedures, fostering a culture of consistency and excellence.

Operational frameworks within an organisation should be designed not only to support but also to enhance the effectiveness of the sales teams. This principle is vital for channel sales partners and a company's internal direct sales force. It's about crafting an environment where sales representatives have the tools, training, and techniques to focus on sales activities that directly impact the customer experience and drive tangible business results. When a business falls short in channel operations and processes, it risks encountering numerous detrimental effects that can impede growth and tarnish its reputation. Inefficiencies or disorganisation in channel management often lead to communication breakdowns, creating confusion and misalignment between the company and its partners. This disarray can spark conflicts and inconsistencies in sales, ultimately leading to diminished customer satisfaction and negative brand perception. A lack of streamlined operations hinders channel partners from accessing essential resources, support, and training, impairing their ability to promote and sell products or services effectively. Additionally, when channel partners are not furnished with clear guidance and defined processes, there's a risk they may deviate from the company's established standards and best practices. This lack of uniformity can lead to a patchwork of customer experiences, as different partners may offer varying service levels, potentially driving customers to seek more consistent and reliable options.

In scenarios of poor channel operations and processes, the ripple effects are manifold: misalignment between the company and its partners, subpar sales performance and a customer experience that lacks uniformity and reliability.

Addressing these challenges is crucial for ensuring a harmonious and productive partnership and maintaining a strong, positive relationship with customers. Businesses must recognise that their operational and process infrastructure is a pivotal factor in their sales channels' overall health and success. By prioritising effective channel operations and processes, companies can nurture a robust, dynamic and customer-focused sales eccsystem, driving partner success and customer satisfaction.

DAVID PARRY

SECTION 3:
Mastering Sales Strategies, Dynamics and Personal Growth

Not to be everyone's favourite grandpa, but sales aren't what they used to be. A lot of the core fundamentals still exist, but the coming of the Internet and the paradigm shift from the product being most important to the customer holding that title have certainly moved the needle a good bit towards a new normal. A lot of the new look of sales from the innovative strategies that define the typical American salesman, a healthy mix of braggadocio and relentless that never sees the sale as "dead" regardless of how many times they've been told nor how many doors – physical or virtual – have been slammed in their faces. But even the rockstar mentality doesn't guarantee individual success. Mick Jagger can still carry a tune at age eighty, but he'll sound warbly and off-beat if the rest of the Stones aren't there to back him up. It takes a village to raise a child and it takes a sales team to succeed in navigating the choppy waters that are out there trying to rough up your boat and keep you reaching those sunny shores of sales. The days of picking up the phone book and dialling until you hit a winner are gone. There is too much competition out there and too many stakeholders to think you can just scoot by on "gut instinct." Becoming a student is the only way forward to becoming a sales master.

Individual Sales Skills and Mindset

The Essence of Change and the Rockstar Mentality

Change, or more precisely, the courage to embrace change, is a vital trait for success. I recall a friend in New York, originally a lawyer from Italy, who decided to change her career path radically. Despite her established position at Ernst & Young in Rome, she chose to pursue acting in New York; not even fluent in English. Her story epitomises the rockstar mentality – tenacity, ambition and the willingness to break barriers. It is a fascinating blend of confidence and egotism, the idea that I can make an impact simply by being "me" to the power that others can barely compute. It is not embraced in many cultures, where teamwork and humility are always the top-drawer qualities, but that doesn't mean it's wrong. People who take over that kind of personality enhancement are there to make an impact, and that's an exciting person to have on your squad. These people make a significant impact in their fields, constantly pushing boundaries and achieving remarkable results.

As a business leader, it's crucial to embody this rockstar mentality. It's about taking ownership, making tough decisions and not shying away from necessary changes. If a team member isn't aligning with the company's vision or delivering expected results, difficult decisions must be made for the company's greater good.

The Tenacity of Rockstar Salespeople

Sales professionals exhibit incredible drive and tenacity in high-performance environments, such as foreign exchange businesses. They understand the importance of persistence and have the knowledge and strategies to excel in their roles. However, this drive is not exclusive to a select few "rockstars." Often, it's about uncovering what motivates each individual and the team. Sometimes, helping one team member overcome a barrier can significantly boost the entire team's performance, creating a ripple effect of motivation and heightened performance.

Prospecting Persistence: The Key to Unlocking B2B Sales

In the B2B realm, perseverance in prospecting can make a significant difference. Any lead, no matter how initially unimpressive, has the potential to culminate in a substantial deal. Relying solely on lead qualification to determine follow-up efforts is a flawed strategy, especially in B2B sales, where the potential value of a lead can be highly variable. A relentless follow-up process, aiming to re-engage prospects multiple times, is essential in capitalising on every opportunity that enters the sales funnel.

Square Pegs in Round Holes: Aligning Skills with Roles

In sales, aligning individual skills with the right roles is crucial for achieving peak performance. A common challenge in enhancing sales team performance is acknowledging when a team member, despite their capabilities, maybe in a misaligned role. For instance, a team member might possess deep subject matter knowledge but lack the inherent skills of a business development (BD) salesperson. Such mismatches often lead to underperformance in critical sales metrics despite the individual's potential in a different role.

The key is recognising where a person's skills can be best utilised. In the example of a team member more suited to an account management role than a BD role, the solution lies in realigning their position to leverage their strengths effectively. Resistance to such changes, often due to tenure or personal likability, can hinder a company's growth and ability to adapt to market demands.

Team Dynamics and Roles

The Importance of Team Dynamics in Mergers

In business mergers, the challenge often extends beyond mere sales growth. It involves unifying diverse groups of people and aligning them with a common goal and journey. Successfully managing a merger is as much about fostering a unified team culture as it is about achieving financial objectives. It requires careful attention to team integration dynamics, ensuring everyone is on board and moving in the same direction.

Whether it's about improving prospecting processes, embracing change, leveraging the power of specialised teams, or managing the complexities of a merger, the underlying principles remain the same. It's about understanding the dynamics of your team, the market, and the importance of specialised roles. By focusing on these aspects, businesses can drive higher performance, better adapt to changes, and achieve sustainable growth. One particularly impactful sales strategy we adopted was the "buddy" system. From day one of making cold calls, we were paired with a "buddy" – someone to learn from or to whom we could smoothly hand off a call if it became too complex. This team approach extended to fieldwork, with one inside salesperson supporting two field sales representatives. In the UK, this translated into someone dedicated to scheduling appointments, offering a brief on the prospect before each meeting, and, crucially, conducting a debrief immediately after every appointment. The inside salesperson promptly logged all insights and outcomes into the CRM system. This methodology was effective and a significant time-saver, streamlining our sales process remarkably.

There were several key learning points and best practices in this sales and business culture that I took forward into my business coaching and consultancy, mainly focusing on the American approach and its application in the UK context:

- Work Ethic and Team Culture. The American business environment, as described, emphasises a blend of high energy and a strong work ethic coupled with a vibrant team culture. This practice of bonding over group activities and maintaining a positive, motivated environment is crucial for team cohesion and morale.

- Persistence and Resilience. Success in this setting was attributed to relentless hard work, long hours and unwavering persistence. This approach underscores the importance of resilience and dedication in achieving business goals.

- Dynamic Sales Techniques. Using a live, interactive whiteboard presentation instead of static PowerPoint slides highlights the value of engaging with the audience and using dynamic sales methods. It emphasises the importance of being adaptable and interactive in sales pitches.

- Anticipating and Addressing Objections. A key strategy was pre-emptively addressing potential client objections within the sales pitch. This proactive approach to good preparation is essential for effective salesmanship and high conversion rates.

- Comprehensive Training and Practice. Rigorous practice sessions and the recording of sales presentations underscore the importance of thorough preparation and continuous improvement in sales techniques.

- The "Buddy" System. Pairing recruits with experienced colleagues facilitates on-the-job learning and provides a support system for handling complex situations. This mentoring approach is beneficial for skill development and knowledge transfer.

- Efficiency in Sales Operations. Debriefing after meetings and immediate data entry into the CRM system highlights the importance of efficiency and organisation in sales operations. This ensures that valuable insights and client information are captured and utilised effectively.

- Adaptability Across Markets. The ability to transfer and adapt these sales strategies from the American context to the UK demonstrates the importance of flexibility and contextual understanding in international business operations.

- Balancing Professional and Personal Interactions. The emphasis on not discussing business during client entertainment showcases the balance required in professional relationships, where personal rapport is just as crucial as business dealings.

These takeaways emphasise a holistic approach to sales and business, where hard work, strategic relationship building, dynamic sales techniques, and continuous learning and adaptation are crucial to success. After reviewing these key learning points and best practices in sales and business culture, particularly focusing on the American approach and its application in the UK context, take a moment to reflect on your professional journey. Consider how these principles could be integrated into your current or future business strategies. Are there aspects of your work ethic, team culture, or sales techniques that could be enhanced based on these insights? How might you apply the "Buddy" system concept in your context? Reflect on balancing professional diligence and personal rapport in your business relationships.

Moving from the dynamic sales techniques and relationship-building strategies in the American and UK markets, my next journey takes us into the intricate world of a large technology distribution and managed services organisation. Here, we see how efficient operations, skills training and strategic partnerships play a pivotal role.

Team-Based Selling: The Power of Collaboration in Complex Sales

Adopting a team-based approach in complex sales, such as software solutions is not just beneficial; it's essential. I recall a client scenario where this approach was crucial. Their sales involved intricate software solutions, demanding more than a single salesperson's expertise. The initial stages involved inside sales teams who identified opportunities and passed them to Business Development (BD) personnel. A more collaborative strategy was imperative when significant opportunities arose, like a potential deal worth upwards of ten million a year over five years.

At this juncture, even though the BD person spearheaded the deal, the company formed a project team right from the onset. This wasn't just about initial customer interactions; it was about foreseeing the complexities down the line and preparing for them meticulously. They brought in experts for scoping, project management, and other vital areas — tasks beyond the typical purview of a BD role. Reflecting on this approach, it becomes increasingly evident how inefficient it is for sales teams to chase down leads single-handedly. For instance, securing just ten leads might involve hundreds of phone calls, not to mention the multiple conversations needed to set an appointment. This immense effort takes valuable time away from actual selling. Similarly, at the end of the sales cycle, the workload doesn't diminish. Once a deal is secured, various operational aspects must be handled - from ensuring the scope aligns with what was sold to the customer to navigating complex contract negotiations often mired in legal intricacies. This comprehensive approach to sales and customer onboarding is crucial, regardless of deal size. Whether a small transaction or a multimillion-dollar contract, the principle remains the same. Every moment spent on non-selling activities is stolen from potential revenue generation. Moreover, the onboarding process should be an opportunity to impress and engage the customer. In one instance, a company demonstrated exceptional onboarding by maintaining consistent communication. However, even in this case, there was room for improvement – a more personal touch, like a phone call, could have further enhanced the experience.

The impact of effective onboarding goes beyond just a smooth transition: It influences referrals, long-term commitments and upsell opportunities. For example, in a project-based scenario like office furniture sales, passing the baton from sales to project management is critical for referrals and customer advocacy.

I've observed a client who exemplified excellence in this area. Their onboarding process was so meticulously structured that it significantly benefited the customer's journey. Yet, the risk of getting this handover wrong is substantial. Without proper onboarding, customers are left with buyer's remorse, questioning where the enthusiastic salesperson disappeared and why they're suddenly receiving impersonal emails from an unknown contact. The key takeaway here is the critical importance of that handover moment. It can make or break the future relationship with the customer regarding referrals, renewals, advocacy, upselling, and more. The transition should be seamless, leaving the customer feeling valued, cared for, and confident in their decision.

In conclusion, striving for best-in-class performance in every aspect of the sales process, especially during onboarding, is not just a goal; it's a necessity. It's about creating a structured, disciplined approach that benefits all parties involved – the customer, the sales team and the organisation as a whole.

The Power of Inside Sales Teams

Consider the example of a leading company in a specific industry, significantly outperforming its competitors. A key to their success is their investment in an inside sales team. While most of their competitors lack such a team, this company employs thirty inside sales representatives. This strategic decision to allocate substantial resources to a dedicated sales team underscores the importance of consistent and focused customer engagement. This approach increases revenue and gives them a formidable edge over competitors.

The Power of Specialised Roles in Sales

The effectiveness of a sales process can be significantly enhanced by assigning specialised roles. For example, a Business Development Representative (BDR) focused on initial engagement and lead nurturing frees the sales representatives to concentrate on closing deals. Once a potential buyer expresses serious interest, the handover to a dedicated salesperson specialising in presentations and closing can streamline the process. This specialisation ensures that each team member plays to their strengths, optimising the entire sales cycle.

After a sale is closed, an effective onboarding

process becomes paramount. A separate team dedicated to onboarding ensures that the customer feels supported and valued, reducing the risk of buyer's remorse and enhancing customer satisfaction. This approach also allows sales representatives to focus on what they do best – selling and closing new deals.

The key to maximising the effectiveness of a sales team lies in recognising the unique skills and strengths of each team member and aligning them with the most suitable roles. Implementing a structured, persistent prospecting process, and assigning specialised roles throughout the sales cycle, from lead generation to onboarding, can significantly enhance performance. Embracing this strategic approach not only optimises the sales process but also ensures that each team member is positioned to contribute their best, driving the business's overall success.

Sales Strategies and Techniques

Prospecting Process: The American Way

In the American approach to prospecting, hard statistics often illuminate the process. For instance, consider a scenario where a hundred companies were approached requesting a callback during a mystery shopping exercise. Remarkably, fifty percent of these companies responded to the initial call. The persistence in follow-up dwindled drastically with each subsequent attempt. By the fourth call, every single company had ceased efforts. This pattern reveals a critical gap in persistence and strategy in prospecting, highlighting a need for a more consistent and determined approach.

The follow-up responsibility is often assigned to sales reps already immersed in closing high-value deals. Expecting them to juggle lead follow-ups while navigating complex negotiations is not just impractical; it's counterproductive. It detracts from their ability to focus on closing significant deals. It's akin to a surgeon being asked to step out from an ongoing surgery to answer phone calls. The need for specialised roles or teams dedicated to different sales process stages becomes glaringly evident here.

The Pitch

Arriving early at a prestigious London address, I was there to meet my competition, fellow contenders all aiming for the same prize — a lucrative consultancy contract with a well-established, large IT company based in Yorkshire. This scene wasn't new to me. Like many companies I had encountered over the years, this one, despite its success and talented team, was experiencing a downturn in profitability due to a commoditised, mature product portfolio and a declining market in its core business area. Yet, there was something distinct about this company. There was an unmistakable air of expectation, excitement, and a palpable determination to succeed. In my weeks of studying the business before this meeting, not a single person I had encountered had anything negative to say about the company, despite some evident frustration over the challenges they faced.

Here was the situation: The prize was a privately-owned PLC, led by an entrepreneurial and successful multimillionaire chairman. He had a reputation for being hands-on and I had not yet had the chance to meet him. The division in question was relatively new – about three years old – and boasted an offering ahead of its time, yet struggling to find its footing in the market.

My first encounter in this endeavour was with the marketing director, a person I had worked with in the morally questionable conglomerate. We shared experiences of corporate bullying, the exploitation of good businesses for short-term gain, and how hardworking people's lives were disrupted by ruthless streamlining – all in the pursuit of short-term profit. These practices were often overlooked by non-executive directors and shareholders, who perhaps were unaware of the true extent of the destruction they were overseeing in their quest for personal and business gains.

This opportunity was different from the others. The passion for the business was evident in everyone I met, from the CEO to the lowest-ranked employee. The CEO, a young, articulate individual with a background in merchant banking and consulting, acted as the main interface between the company and the stock exchange. A tall, young, and fit operations director was deeply entrenched in the mainstream faction at the Northern HQ. His background in sales, meticulous attention to detail and process-driven approach would prove to be key assets for me in the coming months. The finance director, one of the founders of the business, was a cautious, old-style accountant. He might not have had the flamboyance of his multimillionaire co-founder chairman, but he took equal care in building and overseeing this growing empire. He had a penchant for shooting on Mondays and harboured a hidden passion for collecting works of art. Among other key members was a technical expert, a forthright innovator responsible for many leading-edge developments. Unlike his colleagues, he was involved in some slightly dubious business activities ranging from new-age technologies to online gambling and gaming, pay-per-view TV, and other ventures.

My co-presenters and I initially considered collaborating on this project. However, it soon became apparent that our visions were not aligned. One was keen on exploiting this client for short-term gains, a strategy that I believed would lead to failure, especially after meeting the dedicated individuals inside the business. While paying well, this company demanded honest, solid action and tangible results, a philosophy I was not willing to compromise on. Thus, we presented as competitors to the main PLC, executive and non-executive board directors, in what turned out to be a somewhat surreal scenario.

The London office was a modern building in the heart of London's banking district, near the Bank of England. The entrance boasted revolving glass doors, wood-panelled walls, a visitor's couch, potted plants and security personnel who seemed only vaguely interested in the visitors bypassing the prominently placed signage that demanded all visitors show their security passes and sign in at reception. The elevators led to penthouse offices where more couches, potted plants, wood panelling, and high-tech plasma screens rolling images of the business adorned the space. This was an amazing set up with multiple meeting rooms, technology demonstrations and dining areas, all available for their channel partners to use as they wished. These people were absolute professionals in the world of channel management. We were all presented together to the executive and non-executive board. Unfortunately, I was the first to go. I began my presentation by writing a large number on the flip chart, ready to launch into my concise, ten minute pitch on how I planned to help them achieve higher sales, better product positioning and deliver results swiftly. Just as I was about to start, the founder and chairman walked in, his appearance reminiscent of something from the early 1970s – a tall, long-haired gentleman in his late forties, dressed in a relaxed but expensive open-neck white shirt and black trousers, casually holding a small rolled-up cigarette.

Recognising his northern roots and recalling advice from the operations director, I quickly adapted my approach to establish a rapport based on shared regional connections. Ten minutes later, after delivering my pitch, the first of my co-presenters began their presentation, which starkly contrasted mine. They focused on market dynamics, theoretical approaches and significant investments. Their presentation dragged on for more than an hour until, to everyone's surprise, the chairman interrupted midstream with a blunt query about when they planned to get to the point. I couldn't help but grimace, thinking the day was over. After a few more discussion points, we were ushered out of the boardroom. The next day, I received a phone call from the operations director inviting me for a meeting at their northern HQ – exactly the opportunity I had hoped for. It had been almost two years since I left my days in the conglomerate, and I had never doubted my chosen path. Despite the moments of uncertainty about income and leaving the relative comfort of the corporate world, it had all been quite an adventure – so far.

Learning from this sales pitch experience, some of these things sound obvious, but as we all know, what is evident in theory is not necessarily what salespeople do in practice:

- Prepare well in advance. Do the research, create a pitch sheet, get an internal champion where possible and think about their situation and expectations first.

- Know the Company's Culture. It is important to understand what a company believes in and how its team works.
- Adjust to Different Leaders. Different leaders have different styles; adapting to them is good.
- Build Good Relationships. Knowing the right people and having good connections can help in business.
- Communicate Well. Presenting clearly and to the point is very effective, especially with busy executives.
- Keep Up with Trends. Staying updated with new developments in your field is essential.
- Be Professional. Acting professionally is expected in a corporate environment.
- ·Think Fast in the moment. Quickly adjusting your plans in unexpected situations is a valuable skill. Listen to how your prospect reacts to your pitch and adapt.
- Be Patient. Success doesn't always come immediately, so it's important to be patient and keep trying.

SECTION 4:
Why Businesses Fail

Businesses fail every day. Most of them quietly and without much fanfare, pretty much the opposite of how we imagine them. When we think of a business going belly up, we think about Enron back in 2000, its stock flaming away out of control as one ugly Pandora's box after another opened up, revealing that the list of who the company had been lying to basically included everybody. Or of Yahoo, the early Internet leader which twice blew chances to buy Google in its nascent stage and did the same with Facebook before realising it had been hacked so severely that all three billion of Yahoo's members were having their information sold on the Dark Web.

No, most businesses fail for far less spectacular reasons than those listed above. The factors are so simple and so avoidable that it's almost a tragedy to watch them unfold.

Management and Leadership

It all starts at the top, doesn't it? Sometimes, that's also the place to start failing fast, as seen in these reasons:

- Poor Financial Management. Inadequate financial planning, budgeting and cash flow management can quickly lead to business failure. Businesses must clearly understand their financial health and manage resources effectively.

- Funding Issues. Inadequate capital or lack of access to funding can limit a business's ability to invest in growth opportunities or weather financial challenges.

- Ineffective Leadership. Poor leadership, lack of direction and inadequate decision-making can contribute to business failure. Strong leadership is essential for setting goals, motivating teams and making strategic choices.

- Weak Business Model. A flawed business model that doesn't address key value propositions, revenue streams, or cost structures can hinder growth and profitability.

- Inadequate Planning. Insufficient business planning, including lack of a clear business plan, marketing strategy, or growth strategy, can leave a business without a roadmap for success.

- Unhealthy Company Culture. Toxic work environments, lack of employee engagement and poor communication can lead to high turnover rates, reduced productivity and damage to the company's reputation.

- Failure to Adapt. Inability to adapt to changing market conditions, technological advancements, or customer preferences can leave a business behind its competitors.

- Rapid Growth Without Proper Scaling. While growth is desired, growing too quickly without the necessary infrastructure, staffing and resources can lead to operational breakdowns.

Sales and Marketing

No company can withstand a lack of customers or a lack of making more customers. It's simple maths. If no money comes in, your company will soon be on the way out.

- Lack of Market Understanding. Failing to understand the target market's needs, preferences and trends can result in products or services that don't resonate with customers.

- Insufficient Marketing and Sales. Even the best products need effective marketing and sales efforts. Failing to promote products or services effectively can result in low customer acquisition and revenue.

- Competition and Competitive Pressure. Intense competition can erode market share and margins, especially if a business isn't equipped to differentiate itself or respond to rivals effectively.

- Operational Issues. Poor operational processes, supply chain disruptions, or quality control problems can impact customer satisfaction and profitability.

- Technological Disruption. Failing to embrace new

technologies or ignoring digital transformation can render a business obsolete in a fast-evolving marketplace.

External Factors

We all like to point the finger when things don't go our way. In this case, the punishment fits the crime. However, isn't it part of running a business being prepared for the unexpected?

- Legal and Regulatory Challenges. Failure to comply with industry regulations or changes in laws can result in legal troubles and financial penalties.

- Economic Factors. Economic downturns, recessions, or changes in consumer spending habits can significantly impact businesses, especially those with thin profit margins.

Plenty of times, it's not just one thing that dooms a business. Multiple factors interact and have a compounding effect, not unlike taking medicines that shouldn't be taken together. These will greatly accelerate a business's decline and demise. Plenty of times, businesses are struggling internally, and then a tipping point occurs on a broad, macro level, and that's all she wrote. COVID-19 is the low-hanging fruit example in this category, but any sort of economic turnback triggers it, as can more "act of God" incidents like a fire, a flood, a hurricane, or an earthquake. Businesses can try their best to be as redundant as possible against dangerous circumstances, but the truth is that it's not possible to safeguard against everything all at once.

DAVID PARRY

SECTION 5:
Understanding the Business Coaching Logic

Business coaching is an ongoing relationship, it's about helping individuals reach their full potential over time. It's about continuous improvement, working through obstacles and challenges as they arise.

We've made more than a few sporting references on these pages. Think about the likes of Rory Mc Iroy or Michael Jordan. Did they go to a one-time training event and become legends? No, they had ongoing coaching throughout their careers, tweaking their techniques, working on their mindset and constantly striving to improve. The best athletes in the world have coaches, not because the coaches are necessarily better players, but because they provide that consistent external perspective, accountability and the expertise to guide them.

When it comes to business, especially in sales, many think it's just about technique or knowing the product. It's not. It's about understanding human behaviours, how to communicate effectively, how to listen, how to adapt, and how to handle rejection. It's about developing a mindset, understanding the buyer's psychology and always improving. Occasionally a business leader or a managing director believes they can just step in and handle sales because they think it's "easy" or "simple." But it often backfires. Why? Because it's not just about the act of selling. It's about everything that goes behind it — the strategy, the psychology, the resilience, the communication. They are bound to struggle if they've never been trained or coached on those facets. I've seen many managers, especially in smaller businesses, underestimate the complexities of roles like sales, thinking they can easily step into the shoes of a sales director. But without the right insights or coaching, they quickly become overwhelmed.

Coaching is a transformative process and is far more than just holding up a mirror to a business or teaching a methodology. When you enter a company as a consultant, your role goes beyond simply reflecting what the company already knows. It's about shedding light on unseen areas, the shadowed corners where inefficiencies or problems lurk. Good coaching goes beyond merely telling or showing. It involves and immerses the individual in the learning process. "Tell me, and I'll forget. Show me, and I may remember. Involve me, and I'll understand." This is the essence of effective coaching. Coaches ensure that the lessons stick by actively involving individuals in the change process. Coaching is about continuous engagement. It's not about doing the demo for someone and saying, "Look how it's done." Instead, it's about guiding them through the demo and then jointly reviewing and tweaking their approach for better results.

Conclusion

It's an odd role I end up playing from time to time. Sometimes, I come in as the last-ditch effort, the eleventh-hour miracle that might be trying to save something already so far gone that it's all over. Other times, I get there and realise that they're on the verge of a breakthrough; they just don't know what to do next. In either case, I am never the difference-maker, I just shine the light on the forward that presents the best possible option; the real success factor involves the internal dynamics of each company (if they can work together, find their respective strengths and follow the roadmap in front of them).

It's ironic how often they choose to trust me implicitly while holding grudges and suspicions for the coworkers they've known for years or even decades. I'm like the backup goalkeeper for professional football clubs or the backup quarterback if you're an American fan of the NFL. In short, they've seen what the other bloke can do: "Let's give this guy a chance to take the reins and see how it all shakes out." At the end of the day, though, it's never me who will make the dynamic changes that send the company off into its next start of earning success. It starts with a core belief from the very top level on down. If management isn't sold on a deal and utterly committed to it, then it doesn't have a chance of clearing the launchpad. No matter how much technology comes onboard, people will always be the difference-maker. Yes, it takes some extra effort to harness their skillsets correctly, but if you have the right people in house, it's just a matter of time and effort to get them in the right spots. Of course, easier said than done, right? The path is a long and twisty one, starting from the minute you begin cultivating a relationship with someone during the interview process and making sure you are constantly endeavouring not just to do what's in the best interest of the company to maximise productivity but will continue to nurture the success of the individual as well.

Every once in a while, you'll see a company stumble along into a fortune with no idea of how they got it or what they will do with it. It seems to happen more than it does; these companies just seem to get the limelight and a good fifteen minutes of fame as they travel the Internet and worldwide. But these are unicorns in a world where hard and fast plans will always rule the rooster over fly-by-night gamblers. The concept of predictable business performance improvement is fascinating, particularly when examining the trajectory of growth among the businesses I have worked with. Initially, when the first few businesses experienced a surge in growth, it seemed like an unexpected windfall or a fluke. The hard work put into achieving these results often raises the question: Was it luck? However, as this phenomenon was repeated in different businesses and countries, it became apparent that this was not a coincidence. It was a systematic process that yielded growth in hitherto failing companies.

Realising that business growth can be achieved through a repeatable process is intriguing and promising. Witnessing companies and individuals break through their barriers to achieve notable results is not only rewarding but also a testament to the efficacy of these methods. My observation is that most businesses have the potential to evolve and grow, irrespective of their starting point, provided they are equipped with the right team possessing the will and skills to bring about performance improvement. Key, replicable factors that drive the performance of a business from one stage to another have been identified, demonstrating that certain strategies and approaches can lead to consistent success.

Like any successful venture, businesses operate through various stages. Drawing a parallel with a car manufacturer, which progresses from raw material procurement to the final delivery of a finished vehicle, illustrates this journey. Each stage in this process is critical and universally applicable to different business models. Identifying and understanding these stages is the first step in recognising and addressing growth impediments.

Challenges vary across organisations. Some struggle with human resources issues, like talent acquisition or training, while others face hurdles in processes, market understanding, or sales channels. For instance, branding or marketing strategies might fail to resonate with target audiences, or product pricing might not reflect the true value of the offerings.

In the dynamic sales world, the journey towards excellence is continuous, marked by an unending quest for knowledge and skill enhancement. The most proficient sales "rock stars" in any organisation understand that their expertise, no matter how advanced, can always be honed and improved. High-performing teams thrive in environments where learning and improvement are part of the organisational DNA, as seen in global organisations operating across multiple countries. These teams are often the most receptive to new ideas and strategies, constantly seeking ways to refine their approach and outperform their previous achievements. Leadership plays a pivotal role in this process. Effective leaders are those who not only set the vision and strategy for continuous improvement but also actively engage in the learning process themselves. They lead by example, demonstrating a commitment to personal growth and setting the tone for the rest of the team.

The key to sustained success in business lies in recognising that learning and improvement are continuous processes. This ethos, combined with strong values and mutual respect, when ingrained within the fabric of a business culture, becomes the driving force behind achieving and surpassing business objectives, fostering individual growth and elevating the entire organisation to remarkable success.

THE 7 PILLARS

DAVID PARRY

About the Author

David's forty-year career spans teaching to leading multinationals in business recovery and growth. Specialising in performance improvement, he's skilled in planning, process improvement and people development. Passionate about equality, David supports charities and clients with strong values, using his diverse experience in various industries to drive success.

Email: David@davidparry2.co.uk
Author Instagram: davidparry0003

DAVID PARRY

www.ingramcontent.com/pod-product-compliance
Lightning Source LLC
Chambersburg PA
CBHW052150220526
45471CB00004B/1606